CHALLENGING THE PROFESSIONS

CHALLENGING THE PROFESSIONS

Frontiers for rural development

ROBERT CHAMBERS

INTERMEDIATE TECHNOLOGY PUBLICATIONS 1993

Intermediate Technology Publications Ltd
103–105 Southampton Row, London WC1B 4HH, UK

© Intermediate Technology Publications 1993

A CIP record for this book is available from the
British Library

ISBN Paperback 1 85339 194 8
ISBN Hardback 1 85339 208 1

Typesetting by Inforum, Rowlands Castle, Hants
Printed by SRP Exeter

Contents

Tables

Illustrations

Preface

Challenging the Professions questions the dominant approaches of professions, disciplines and bureaucracies concerned with rural development. The theme is that 'we', who call ourselves professionals, are much of the problem, and to do better requires reversals of much that we regard as normal. The challenge is to upend our thinking, to turn values on their heads, to invent and adopt new methods, and to behave differently. The frontiers are personal and professional, requiring changes which are radical but quite surprisingly practicable: to question our values; to be self-critically aware; to see simple as often optimal; to offset our spatial and seasonal biases; to help rural people do their own analyses; to stay in villages and learn from and with rural people; to test and use participatory approaches, methods and procedures; to encourage decentralization and diversity; to put people before things, and poor people first of all.

To face these challenges both threatens and exhilarates. It threatens the snug security of citadels of learning with their traditional textbooks, tread-mill teaching, conservative curricula, and assurance of timeless knowledge. It exhilarates because these citadels are also prisons. To break out, learning to unlearn, embracing doubt, and welcoming uncertainty, is a liberation. The shifts from things to people, from central control to local initiative, from standardization to diversity, open up new opportunities and potentials. For rural development professionals, these make the 1990s, and the twenty-first century beyond, a privileged time to be alive.

In selecting, editing and writing the papers for the eight chapters in this book, I have tried to capture and convey some of the challenge and excitement of these changes. I have weighed four criteria: relevance to the theme; normal neglect of the angle or topic; practical implications for future research, policy and action; and known demand for the material by teachers, trainers, researchers and practitioners. Before the publication of this book, most of the papers were difficult or expensive to obtain or had not been written in their present form. The aim here is to make them more accessible, especially to professionals and students in the South. Any reader who finds the book of interest and use may wish to join me in thanking Intermediate Technology for the low price which makes the book more widely affordable and available.

For future action, each chapter presents its own professional frontier. Chapter by chapter, the challenges are:

1. to all concerned with rural development, to recognise normal professional thinking, values, methods and behaviour as much of the problem, and a new professionalism of reversals as much of the solution;

2. to planners, bureaucrats and academics alike to recognize practical principles and modes of thought, and the potential for change from new procedures which are simple, participatory, and sparing in demands on staff time;

3. to economists, planners and aid agency staff to recognize and practice 'simple is optimal', to decentralize in identifying poverty-focused projects, and to improve their judgement by spending time personally in the field;

4. to policymakers, practitioners, academics and researchers, to be aware of and mitigate adverse seasonality, especially interactions of health and agriculture in tropical wet seasons, and to encourage and enable participatory analysis of seasonality in each location;

5. to agricultural researchers and extensionists, to reverse learning, locations and roles with farmers, to provide them with baskets of choices, and to support diversity and complexity in farming systems;

6. to all concerned with projects, to counterbalance engineers' and economists' normal preoccupation with infrastructure, budgets, targets and schedules, and to support learning projects which are unhurried, adaptive and flexible, without pressure to spend, and with continuity of committed staff in the field;

7. to NGOs and those who fund them, to assess NGOs' comparative competence for making a difference and to identify and exploit their potential for wider impacts, especially through developing and spreading new approaches and methods;

8. to policymakers, practitioners and academics alike, to avoid the pitfalls of both neo-Fabian and neo-liberal ideology, and to adopt in their place an ideology of reversals, a practical pluralism which seeks to dismantle the disabling state and to enable and empower the poor.

I have shortened chapter 1, lightly edited chapters 2, 3, 4, 6 and 8, and rewritten much of chapters 5 and 7. To chapter 4 I have added a postscript listing some major contributions to the study of tropical seasonality during the past decade. For ease of reading and for relevance, I have in some places changed the syntax, especially the tenses of verbs, but I have resisted the temptation to rewrite substantially. Readers are asked to note that had I done so, there would have been more emphasis on participation in chapter 2.

This book is, then, addressed to all who are concerned with rural poverty and rural development, whatever their discipline or profession. It is equally for researchers, policymakers, students and faculty of universities, colleges and training institutes, and the headquarters and field staff of government departments, NGOs and aid agencies. It is designed to be relevant, readable and manageable. Each chapter has an abstract at its head. This should give the reader an overview in a matter of minutes, allowing an informed choice of what and what not to read. The chapters are arranged as a sequence for teaching, for reading, or for discussion.

The enduring challenge is to continue to question normal professional concepts, values, methods and behaviour. Let me hope that this book, however modestly, will provoke and encourage readers to be critical, to question convention, to learn from past errors, omissions and achievements, to go further than the points reached here, and then to share their insights. For through sharing criticism, doubt, ideas and experience, as this book tries to do, we may find ways of doing less badly in the struggle for a better world.

Acknowledgements

Those who contributed to the original papers, through typing, editing, comments and criticism, are too numerous to name; but I thank them all. I am grateful to Linda Bateman at IDS for putting most of the papers onto disc, and to Helen McLaren for help, advice and the infectious spirit of Zen with which she has contributed to the later stages in editing and producing the text.

Where chapters have been published before, I gratefully acknowledge permission from the publishers for them to be reprinted, as follows:

Chapter 1: 'Normal Professionalism, New Paradigms and Development' is from *IDS Discussion Paper* 227, December 1986, of the same title; also in Edward Clay and John Shaw (ed.), *Poverty, Development and Food: Essays in honour of H.W. Singer on his 75th birthday*, Macmillan Press, Basingstoke and London, 1987, pp 229–53.

Chapter 2: 'Managing Rural Development: Procedures, Principles and Choices' is from the final chapter of *Managing Rural Development: Ideas and Experience from East Africa*, first published by The Scandinavian Institute of African Studies, Uppsala, in 1974, and then republished by Kumarian Press, West Hartford, Connecticut in 1985. (The book as a whole is going out of print but will be obtainable from the University of Michigan Out of Print Books on Demand Program.)

Chapter 3: 'Project Selection for Poverty-Focused Rural Development: Simple is Optimal' was published in *World Development* vol. 6 no. 2, pp 209–19, 1978.

Chapter 4: 'Health, Agriculture and Rural Poverty: Why Seasons Matter' had several revisions, with incarnations in: Kerr L. White and Patricia Bullock (eds) *The Health of Populations*, The Rockefeller Foundation, 1980; as *IDS Discussion Paper* No 148, 1979 and in *The Journal of Development Studies* vol. 18 no. 2, 1982, pp 217–38.

Chapter 5: 'Farmer-First: A Practical Paradigm for the Third Agriculture' is from Miguel Altieri and Susan B. Hecht (eds), *Agroecology and Small Farm Development*, CRC Press Inc. 1991, which was revised with additional material as Robert Chambers and Camilla Toulmin 'Farmer-First: Achieving Sustainable Dryland Development in Africa', in Margaret Haswell and Diana Hunt (eds), *Rural Households in Emerging Societies: Technology and change in Sub-Saharan Africa*, Berg, Oxford and New York, 1991, pp 23–48.

Chapter 6: 'Normal Professionalism and the Early Project Process: Problems and Solutions', appeared as *IDS Discussion Paper* 247, July 1988.

Chapter 7: 'Thinking about NGOs' Priorities: Additionality and Spread', is rewritten from two papers: 'Thinking about NGOs' Priorities', background paper for the OXFAM Workshop on Arid Lands Management, Cotonou, Benin, 23–27 March 1987; and 'Spreading and Self-Improving: A Strategy for Scaling Up', in Michael Edwards and David Hulme (ed.), *Making a Difference: NGOs and development in a changing world*, Earthscan, London (1992); and new material has been added.

Chapter 8: 'The State and Rural Development: Ideologies and an Agenda for the 1990s' is *IDS Discussion Paper* 269, November 1989, also published in Christopher Colclough and James Manor (eds), *States or Markets? Neoliberalism and the development policy debate*, Clarendon Press, Oxford 1991 pp 260–78.

For comments on a draft of chapter 7 I thank Jurjen van der Tas.

At various times and in various places, the work on which this book is based has been supported by the Aga Khan Foundation, the Ford Foundation, OXFAM, the Overseas Development Administration, the Rockefeller Foundation, and the Swedish International Development Agency. The usual disclaimers apply, and responsibility for errors, omissions and opinions is mine alone.

Finally, I thank my colleague Mick Moore at the Institute of Development Studies without whose imaginative support this book would not have been completed.

ROBERT CHAMBERS
12 February 1993

Abbreviations

CBA	cost-benefit analysis
CDR	complex, diverse and risk-prone. See also the third agriculture
CIAT	Centro Internacional de Agricultura Tropical, Apartado Aereo 6713, Cali, Colombia, fax: (57) 23–647243
FF	farmer-first, referring to the new complementary paradigm of agricultural research and extension that reverses the learning and locations of TOT, with farm families playing a major part in technology development and choice
FPR	farmer participatory research
GR	green revolution
ICLARM	International Center for Living Aquatic Resource Management, PO Box 1501, Makati, Metro Manila 1299, Philippines, tel: (63–2) 818–0466 or 818–9283, fax: (63–2) 816–3183, telex: 45658 ICLARM PM
ICRISAT	International Crops Research Institute for the Semi-Arid Tropics, Patancheru, Andhra Pradesh 502 324, India, tel: 842 224016, fax: 842–241239
IDS	the Institute of Development Studies, University of Sussex, Brighton BN1 9RE, England, tel: 273–606261, fax: 273–621202 or 691647, telex: 877997 IDSBTN G
IFPRI	International Food Policy Research Institute, 1776 Massachusetts Avenue NW, Washington DC 20036, USA, tel: 202–862–5600, fax: 202–467–4439, telex: 440054
IIED	International Institute for Environment and Development, 3 Endsleigh Street, London WC1H 0DD, tel: 071–388–2117, fax: 071–388–2826
ILEIA	Information Centre for Low External Input Agriculture, PO Box 64, 3830 AB Leusden, The Netherlands, tel: 33–943086, fax: 33–940791, telex: 79380 ETC NL
IMF	International Monetary Fund
IRR	internal rate of return

IRRI	International Rice Research Institute, PO Box 933, Manila, Philippines, tel: 63–2–884869, fax:63–2–8178470
ISNAR	International Service for National Agricultural Research Management, PO Box 93375, 2509 AJ The Hague, The Netherlands, tel: 31–70–3496100, fax: 31–70–3819677
NDUAT	Narendra Dev University of Agriculture and Technology, Kumar Ganj, Faizabad, Uttar Pradesh, India
NERAD	Northeast Rainfed Agriculture Development Project
NGO	Non-government organization
ODA	Overseas Development Administration of the British Government, 94 Victoria Street, London SW1E 5JL, tel: 071–917–7000, fax: 071–917–0425
ODI	Overseas Development Institute, Regent's College, Inner Circle, Regent's Park, London NW1 4NS, tel: 071–487–7413, fax: 071–487–7590, telex: 94082191 ODIUK
OECD	Organization for Economic Co-operation and Development, tel: 33–5248293
PBSA	planning by successive approximation
PRA	participatory rural appraisal
PTD	participatory technology development
RRA	rapid rural appraisal
RWG	redistribution with growth
SSA	sub-Saharan Africa
SUAN	the Southeast Asian Universities' Agroecosystems Network
TOT	transfer of technology
T and V	Training and Visit, a system of agricultural extension promoted by the World Bank

Definitions

green
revolution
agriculture

the agriculture of fertile and well-watered areas in the South, notably the irrigated plains and deltas of Asia (Chapter 5, Table 1)

industrial
agriculture

the agriculture of the temperate and rich North, with high inputs and subsidies (Chapter 5, Table 1)

new
professionalism

thinking, values, methods and behaviour which reverse many elements of normal professionalism

normal
professionalism

the thinking, values, methods and behaviour dominant in professions and disciplines and reflecting 'core' or 'first' biases

the North

the richer, more industrialized countries mainly in the temperate northern hemisphere

paradigm

a coherent and mutually supporting pattern of concepts, values, methods and action, amenable to wide application

the South

the poorer, more agricultural countries mainly in the tropics

the third
agriculture

the variously complex, diverse and risk-prone (CDR) agriculture of the South, mainly rainfed and on undulating land, found in hinterlands, mountains, hills, wetlands, and the semi-arid, subhumid and humid tropics (Chapter 5, Table 1)

transfer of
technology

the normal basic paradigm of agricultural research and extension in which priorities are decided by scientists and funding bodies, and new technology is developed on research stations and in laboratories and then handed over to extension to transfer to farmers

1 Normal Professionalism, New Paradigms and Development

You are old, Father William, the young man said,
And your hair has become very white
And yet you incessantly stand on your head–
Do you think, at your age, it is right?

Lewis Carroll, *Alice in Wonderland*

This chapter argues that though development realities and fashions change fast, normal professionalism – the thinking, values, methods and behaviour dominant in a profession or discipline – is stable and conservative. It is linked with core-periphery structures of power and knowledge, reproduced through teaching and defended by specialization. It values and rewards 'first' biases which are urban, industrial, high technology, male, quantifying, and concerned with things and with the needs and interests of the rich.

The new professionalism reverses the values, roles and power relations of normal professionalism. It puts people first and poor people first of all. The 'last-first' paradigm includes learning from the poor, decentralization, empowerment, local initiative, and diversity. Development is not by blueprint but by a flexible and adaptive learning process. To achieve reversals on a massive scale is now perhaps the greatest challenge facing the development professions.

Context

In the mid-1980s, when this chapter was written, the morbid preoccupation of development studies looked more than ever justified. Despite some big gains in health and education, the scale and awfulness of deprivation, especially among the poorer rural people of the south, remained an outrage. Development studies, theories and practice were caught off their guard as more countries, and more people than perhaps ever before, were trapped in downward drifts. The rate of obsolescence of development fashions and ideas had accelerated. Some passed so fast that, as with the unsuccessful mountaineers on Rum Doodle (Bowman, 1956), high altitude deterioration set in before acclimatization was complete: prescriptions and policies were abandoned before they had time to adapt and improve in the light of mistakes and experience. We seemed never to get there, or get there in time. We were always late, and always out-of-date. But against the gloom and frenetic rise and fall of fashions could be set one steady trend which augured well: the gradual emergence of a new set of ideas about the theory and practice of development, especially, but not only, in rural

1

development. These were cohering into a new pattern. They generated new agendas for research and action. They demanded and supported the new paradigm and the new professionalism which are basic themes in this book, and about which this chapter was written.

Development paradigms and professions

A new development paradigm is taking form. I use the word paradigm to mean a coherent and mutually supporting pattern of concepts, values, methods and action, amenable to wide application. Some of the 'new' in the paradigm is old, having been part of development thinking for some time. What is especially new is that hitherto separate strands and tendencies are fitting into a clearer and more powerful pattern. The old development paradigms have left much to be desired. The question now is whether the new one can succeed in those domains where the old ones have failed.

Any discussion of paradigms invites reference to Thomas Kuhn's illumination of normal science in his book *The Structure of Scientific Revolutions* (1962). Kuhn used 'paradigm' in a restricted sense, to mean 'universally recognised scientific achievements that for a time provide model problems and solutions for a community of practitioners' (Kuhn, 1962:x). Kuhn's universe of sciences was consciously limited to the physical ones such as astronomy, physics and chemistry. In development, however, these are entirely or largely irrelevant, whereas biology, engineering, medicine, and the social sciences are involved in both research and action. Three contrasts between the development professions and sciences and Kuhn's physical sciences are worth noting:

- a changing reality: for the physical (and also biological) sciences there is a strong, though not unchallenged (see Sheldrake, 1985), assumption that the basic reality does not change, whereas in the development social sciences not only does the reality constantly change (compare sub-Saharan Africa 1985 with 1970), but the rate of change seems to be accelerating;
- new ideas derived from experience: the driving force for change in the physical sciences comes from anomalies and from technologies for observation, measurement and reductionist analysis. In the development field the driving force comes much more from changing reality and from action and experience;
- tolerance of competing ideas: in the biological and social sciences competing paradigms can coexist more easily over long periods (Lamarckian and Darwinian, and neo-Lamarckian and neo-Darwinian, theories of evolution; Marxist and neo-classical theories in economics) whereas in the physical sciences more universal paradigm shifts normally take place within a generation.

Rapid changes in reality and the lack of widely accepted stable paradigms can lead observers to suppose that development thought and practice are themselves unstable. At two levels this is indeed true.

The first, less important instability is in academic fashions. Changes continue but were more marked and frantic in the 1950s and 1960s when

2

academic luxuries could better be afforded. Many fashions had brief lives. In the social sciences, new development subjects ballooned – the diffusion of innovations, systems theory in political science, the development administration movement, the mode of production debate – with exponential explosions of erudite articles, until those paper dinosaurs sank out of sight, dragged down by the weight of their footnotes.

The second instability, much more significant, is policy prescriptions for economic development. Sharp shifts in conventional wisdom over short periods are symptoms of a struggle to keep up with diverse and rapidly changing conditions and to learn from experience, as stress on policy dialogue, restructuring and market forces has illustrated. Whatever else may be uncertain, one can predict with reasonable confidence that ideas about development policy in less-developed countries will continue to change fast, and that by the end of the century they will be very different from today.

In such fluid conditions, the use of the word paradigm, with its sense of formal and stable relationships, may be questioned. In the social sciences it is more customary to talk of networks and discourses which accommodate shifts of meaning and content. I shall retain the word paradigm because my argument is that underneath or alongside the sudden switches of vocabulary and the lurches of policy, a new, coherent and consistent set of ideas about development, and especially about rural development practice, has been emerging almost independently, as though in another dimension; and that its gathering support and influence have been partly concealed by the overlays of rhetoric and transient policy debate at the macro level.

It is also overlaid and hidden by another, more powerful, stable continuity which survives passing academic fashions and rapid changes in policy wisdom. This is to be found in the practical professional side of development and its teaching. This stability has links with academic disciplines and is entrenched in and sustained by the development professions working in government departments. It is part of what I shall call normal professionalism, where each profession can be said to have its normal paradigm.

Normal professionalism

Normal professionalism refers to the thinking, values, methods and behaviour dominant in a profession or discipline. There is some analogy with Kuhn's normal science which he saw as 'a strenuous and devoted attempt to force nature into the conceptual boxes supplied by professional education' (Kuhn, 1962:5). Like normal science, normal professionalism is conservative. In the development professions, however, normal professionalism encompasses much more than normal science: for it is concerned not just with research, but with action; and its actors are not just in research institutes and universities, but also international and national organizations, most of them in specialized departments of government (administration, agriculture, animal husbandry, community development, cooperation, education, finance, fisheries, forestry, health, irrigation, justice, planning, public works, water development, and so on). Normal professionalism is a worldwide phenomenon, and has built-in stability from its link

3

with knowledge and power, reverence for established method, capacity to reproduce itself, and defences against threat. It is sustained by the core-periphery structure of knowledge and knowledge generation, by education and training, by organizational hierarchy, and by rewards and career patterns. Let us examine these in turn.

The core-periphery structure of knowledge and knowledge-generation is so universal that it is habitually overlooked. Those who seek advancement in life seek education and training, and look inwards and upwards for enlightenment and reward. In their careers they move geographically inward to larger and larger urban cores, and simultaneously upward in organizational hierarchies. The capacity to generate knowledge, and the power that goes with that, rise on the gradients from peripheries to cores. Professional rewards (the Nobel prizes being the most extreme example) stem from and reflect the values of the cores, and attract and orient peripheral aspirants like iron filings to their magnets. Normal professionalism is embodied in the norms, methods and behaviours which are taught, learnt, and rewarded. At the university stage, textbooks are the stone tablets of normal professionalism; later journals and the real or supposed policies of journal editors become more significant, together with promotion boards and professional associations.

Conservatism

The process is conservative. The diploma disease (Dore, 1976) drives students to seek degrees or certificates as tickets for jobs and upward movement, and ensures devoted and strenuous learning of whatever is in the textbooks or taught in the classroom. Value is placed on methods for doing things, and then correct observance of those methods. Wherever possible, in deference to the 'hard' sciences and the power of mathematics, these methods involve numbers. Methods are stable. Where they are mathematical and lend themselves to ritual repetition, they are easily accepted and perpetuated. The more they rely on counting and statistics the more methods endure. They survive both because they are useful and because they provide psychological security for those who practice them. So economists learn social cost-benefit analysis; civil engineers learn rules of design; sociologists learn to prepare and analyse questionnaire surveys; agricultural scientists learn to design and lay out experimental plots; psychologists learn to test intelligence and other psychological attributes. Equipped with knowledge of correct methods, those who pass upwards in the system feel confident that they know what to do; and assume, as good normal professionals, that the exercise of their learnt skills will establish truth, if they do research, or lead to right actions, if they are involved in development.

Conservatism can also occur in the form of peripheral fossilization. This is built into core-periphery relations, career patterns, and the hierarchy of training. Sometimes teachers lecture to their students from their own old notes. They hang onto their old textbooks for security. Teaching is then reproduced through successive generations. Staff from Third World uni-

4

versities who have in the past been trained in the West (or East) have returned home to relative isolation with the ideas, orthodoxies, and fashions of those particular years which some then have reproduced for the remainder of their academic lives. Institutions, with their huge inertia, preserve these geological traits. Some Departments of Extension Education in Indian Agricultural Universities, for example, teach concepts and concerns about diffusion of innovations that were current in the late 1950s and 1960s when their now senior staff spent time in American universities. Today (1986), the book and journal famine in much of SSA is having a similar effect, for different reasons, and with terrible demoralization of university and other staff: it was reported in 1985 that the University of Nairobi had not been able to order books for five years, the University of Dar es Salaam for seven years, and the University of Makerere for thirteen years. An external examiner at Makerere described his experience as entering a time warp, to read essays about the economic theories of earlier decades. The tragic irony of these effects is that debates about development become incestuously North-North (like the many meetings in the UK in 1985 about sub-Saharan Africa), and conservative normal professionalism itself develops a core-periphery gradient: the poorer the country and the more isolated its professionals from the rest of the world, the more behind the times (as defined by some in the core) and the more normal its professionals are liable to be.

Defences

Normal professionalism also maintains itself through a repertoire of defences against discordance and threat. It seeks security through specialization, simplification, rejection, and assimilation.

The first defence is specialization. This has dimensions of subject and of physical territory. Foresters stick to trees, and moreover to trees in the forests and forest plantations which they control. Animal specialists stick to animals – the animals about which they have been trained. Agricultural scientists stick to crops, those in which they have specialized. Civil engineers in irrigation stick to design and construction, with a little maintenance, and hold back from operation and management. In such ways, only the familiar is faced. Professions are inbred and look inwards. Normal is narrow.

Simplification is also a defence by limiting concerns and criteria. It often takes the form of a single measure or criterion: the single numeraire that consummates cost-benefit analysis; the single objective of 'production' so often proclaimed by agricultural scientists; the achievement of physical targets by civil engineers, or foresters, or water developers; water-use efficiency (Bos and Nugteren, 1974) by irrigation managers and analysts. But as Oscar Wilde once said, 'Truth is never pure and rarely simple': the real world is complex; objectives are multiple; paths of change are not undirectional, and they cannot be predetermined. The single objective or measure gives some security but the many-sided nature of physical and human reality is difficult to keep permanently shut out. So other defences are also needed.

One of these is rejection, taking various forms, including ridicule, even

5

persecution, and boundary definition and maintenance. The best known examples come from the history of science: the persecution of Galileo; the scorn poured by geophysicists on Wegener's theory of continental drift; the definition of parapsychology as being 'unscientific' despite the exceptional scientific rigour of its methods (Barnes, 1982:90–3): and, more recently the editorial in *Nature* on Sheldrake's theory of formative causation (which explains anomalies and invites scientific testing) (Sheldrake, 1985:221–3), headed 'A book for burning?' The major comparable rejection by the development professions is of the validity of the knowledge of rural people, or indigenous technical knowledge (ITK) (IDS 1979 ; Brokensha *et al.*, 1980). Many professionals cannot believe that poor rural people can know anything of consequence. Wegener's theory may have been rejected by geophysicists partly because Wegener earned most of his living as a meteorologist;[1] ITK is rejected because those who possess it are worse, not even professionals, but illiterate, of low status and poor.

A final normal professional defence against threat or difficulty is assimilation, using familiar methods to modify, describe and often put some sort of number to the discordance, coding it so that it can be fitted on as an extension of the normal paradigm. The familiar formal method then remains paramount by transforming and incorporating the problem. This can be found in every discipline which aspires to hardness. Thus economists respond to the challenge of differential social effects through weightings and shadow pricing; irrigation engineers respond to poor performance on canal irrigation systems by extending physical works, which they know how to construct, to lower and lower parts of the system; doctors respond to the charge that they serve only urban elites by extending health clinics to provide curative services to rural areas.

In all these instances, the response is 'normal'. It does not threaten the paradigm; instead it extends and even reinforces it. Social cost-benefit analysis takes longer and requires more data but ends up with the same familiar percentages and ratios. Irrigation engineers have more work to do but it is of the same kind. Doctors have larger networks of curative institutions to manage, and armies of health workers to train, but they fit into a hierarchy of medical competence and specialization in which each level deals with what it can, and refers the more professionally-exacting cases upwards, reaffirming and reinforcing professional authority.

In ways like these, normal responses maintain or enhance professional power. Reproduced through training and rewards, conservative and well-defended, normal professionalism is very stable.

Weaknesses

Normal professionalism has virtues. Civil Engineers do build dams, usually with considerable technical success; doctors do cure the sick. But much is wrong. Three weaknesses illustrate parts of a larger syndrome: gaps; misuse of methods; and prior bias.

The 'core' nature and specialization of disciplines and professions combine to leave gaps when they are applied in peripheries. Professions have been generated in core conditions to fit core categories and handle core interests and problems. More is known by professionals about the things of the rich than about the things of the poor. Main-line disciplinary work in, say, agriculture, animal husbandry or forestry has in the past fitted the needs of those who are better off and the benefits have been largely appropriated by them. The gaps left by normal professionalism often correspond with the resources and interests of the poor where the potentials of modern science have been little applied. So new 'last' technology and new patterns of gap development offer scope for enabling poor rural people to command better livelihoods.

Specialization reinforces the neglect of 'last' gaps. There is a core elitist assumption that if enough disciplines are mustered and all put to work to study a rural situation or problem in their normal professional way, it will be fully covered. Like searchlights, they will, if there are enough of them, shed dazzling light on all of the target. But this is not so. One example can suffice. Agro-forestry – the growing of trees in interaction with crops and/or animals – is a major component in the farming systems of hundreds of millions of poor farmers. But professional forestry is concerned with trees in forests, agricultural sciences with crops, and animal sciences with animals. There has been no discipline or recognised profession of agro-forestry. The journal *Agroforestry Systems* is only a few years old. ICRAF – the International Council for Research in Agroforestry – has been denied membership of the Consultative Group for International Agricultural Research, and in 1985 had only some 18 scientists for the whole world.[†] Agro-forestry is a low status activity, the responsibility either of a junior forester isolated in a Ministry of Agriculture, or of a junior agricultural scientist in a Ministry of Forests, or of no one at all. As with agroforestry, so in general, disciplines, professions and departments are so organized and interlocked that gaps between them have low priority and low status.

Misuse of method is another weakness of normal professionalism. Often misuse makes it possible to manage political pressures; often too, misuse represents the exercise of informal power under the guise of technical objectivity. Canal irrigation transmission losses and social cost-benefit analysis present two parallels. Those designing a canal irrigation system are often under political pressure to irrigate a distant area: in one case in India, to accommodate such pressure, the assumption was simply made that there would be no transmission losses, although they often run at 50 per cent or more. Irrigation was made possible on paper and the real problem deferred. Similarly, those responsible for social cost-benefit analysis often face political pressure to produce an acceptable internal rate of return so that a project can qualify for funding. It is easy (though not in the textbooks) to alter assumptions about speed of implementation, volume of future production, and future prices, to produce whatever internal rate of return is required. Both irrigation design engineers and economists appraising projects are thus able to bend to political pressures, while at the

[†] Author's note. Subsequently ICRAF was expanded considerably and admitted to the CGIAR.

7

same time, through the inaccessibility of their calculations and assumptions, maintaining some autonomy and power.

The law of prior bias is another weakness of normal professionalism. According to this, what comes first stands highest, gets most, and sets patterns. This has been enormously influential in development thinking, with mutual reinforcement between overlapping sequences: industrialization before agriculture in early post-second world war development theory and practice; infrastructure before agricultural and rural development in the evolution of priorities of the World Bank; and the sequence of appraisal, design and construction before operation in every project, even in agriculture. Thus we have hardware before software; and construction before operation. Mathematical skills are also more needed and more used in these earlier stages than in the later ones. Much of this is necessary and inevitable, but the effects are profound and lasting. For methods and patterns developed for the early (hardware, construction, physical) activities persist into and dominate the later (software, operational, social) stages.

These limitations in normal professionalism are only what is revealed by a core-periphery, centre-outwards view. There is another – reversed, periphery-core, outside to centre – view which reveals much more. To understand this we need to examine polar contrasts between what is core or 'first' and what is peripheral or 'last'.

Polar paradigms: first and last

Power, wealth, knowledge and professionalism are intimately linked. In individual perception, choice and behaviour, deep biases operate. The poles which professionals normally embrace I shall call 'core' or 'first', and those which they normally reject I shall call peripheral or 'last'. These deep biases are not universal. I posit them not as universal laws, but as general tendencies. They can be presented in Table 1.1.

Table 1.1:   Deep preferences of normal professionals

Core or First	Peripheral or Last
power	weakness
comfort	discomfort
wealth	poverty
core location	peripheral location
urban	rural
industrial	agricultural
things	people
clean, odourless	dirty, smelly
standarised	diverse
tidy	untidy
controlled	uncontrolled
certainty	doubt

Normal professionals gravitate towards the core list.

8

Linked and partly overlapping with these deep preferences are preferences for technology (see Table 6.1).

These preferences are embodied in a basic ideology in which development is seen as a movement along gradients from peripheral or last towards core or first, and through the spread of core conditions into peripheries. So industry has been valued more than agriculture, large-scale agriculture than small-scale, coffee than cassava, tractors than bullocks or human power, exotic cattle than indigenous, and cattle more than goats, hens or bees. Development has been seen as a process of growth stimulated by transfer of technology, a transfer in one direction, from rich and powerful to poor and weak, from first to last.

The new professionalism reverses power relations – 'putting the last first' – in choice of clients, professional values, research methods, and roles. Clients are the poorer and the more deprived, and especially those in rural areas. Professional values are turned around, with shifts towards 'low' technology and software. Research approaches and methods are more holistic and experimental, and located more in field conditions. Roles are reversed, with poor people as teachers and experimenters. Research priorities are determined not by scientists but by the poor themselves. Evaluation is not by peers but by clients. And not surprisingly, the status of many new professionals in the eyes of their peers, is low, if not off the bottom of the scale altogether.

Such reversals may appear extreme. If all professionals adopted them, the modern world as we know it might cease to hold together. There is, though, little danger of that. The point is that whole professional systems are so powerfully biased, that a balance will never be achieved unless many, many resolutely make these reversals. To do so requires strong efforts to offset the pull of trained reflexes, normal incentives, and personal convenience. New professionals who make such reversals have already done much, for example in community medicine, nutrition, agricultural economics and agricultural research. But most of the need remains unmet and most of the potential untapped. There are many reasons for this. But the reason of respectability is weaker now than before; for these reversals now fit and are reinforced by an emerging new paradigm of development which is commanding more and more support.

The new development paradigm

No short statement can do justice to the new development paradigm which has emerged and is taking shape in the development professions. Nor can I do more than provide a personal sketch, starting with some of its origins in both negative and positive experience.

On the negative side, there is the long experience of failures of first/last approaches for the poorer people, especially the poorer rural people. Yet another catalogue is unnecessary. It has been well enough documented that first/last biases which are variously urban, industrial, capital-intensive, centralized, high technology, and planned top-down often leave poor people out or make things worse for them. Curative medicine, on-station agricultural research, parastatals, co-operatives, subsidized agricultural equip-

9

ment, centrally administered credit programmes – these and many other initiatives favour the less-poor.

On the positive side, many experiences point towards similar conclusions. The experiences include health programmes – WHO's health for all and UNICEF's GOBI, (growth charts, oral rehydration, breast feeding and immunization), both of which explicitly seek to reach and empower the poorer people, especially women and children; avant-garde approaches in agricultural research (e.g. Matlon *et al.*, 1984; Ashby, 1984; Rhoades and Booth, 1982; Rhoades, 1984a and b) which seek to enable poor farmers to identify research priorities and retain initiative as collaborators in the technology development process (see Chapter 5 for further developments); initiatives of voluntary and some government agencies in catalysing the formation of groups which then exercise effective demands; and the finding that people do more for themselves than expected when they command resources and control their environment. Perhaps the most significant and influential experience, though, has been in South and Southeast Asia with the initiatives which generated the idea of the learning process approach to development (Korten, 1980, 1984a and b; Bagadion and F. Korten, 1985).

The new development paradigm has four interacting levels: normative; conceptual; empirical; and practical.

The *normative* level is simple: development should be people-centred (Korten and Klauss 1984; Cernea 1985); people come before things; and poorer people come before the less poor. It is right to put the last first, to give priority to those who are more deprived – the poor, physically weak, vulnerable, isolated and powerless, and to help them change those conditions. It is also right to enable them to identify and demand what they want and need.

The normative level thus supports the reversals of the new professionalism. Women come before men, and children before adults. The weak come before the strong. Professionals become not experts but learners, and poor people their teachers. Priorities are not those projected by professionals, but those perceived by the poor. The goal of development is not growth as defined by normal professionals, but well-being as defined by the poor for themselves. Poor people will define their well-being in different ways. Many are likely to want livelihoods more than employment (Chambers, 1983, 1986) where livelihoods mean adequate assets, food, and cash for physical and social well-being, and security against impoverishment; and they are likely to emphasize both health and consumption. But their priorities will never be uniform.

At the *conceptual* level, development is not a progress in a single direction, but a process of continuous adaptation, problem-solving and opportunity – exploiting under pressure. Causality is complex and circular, not simple and lineal (Jamieson, 1987). Development is not movement towards a fixed goal but continuous adaptation to maximise well-being in changing conditions.

At the *empirical* level, there are four verifiable elements:

(i) *conditions are diverse and complex.* Physically, environments contain much variation. Resource-poor farms contain, create and exploit

10

micro-environments. Resource-poor farming is usually more diverse in its crop-livestock-tree interrelations and its use of biomass than resource-rich farming. Poorer people are often 'foxes' with many different enterprises with which they cobble together a livelihood, doing different things at different seasons, in contrast with better-off people who are more often 'hedgehogs', with one major life support. Diversity and complexity are usually greater for the poorer than for the less poor.

(ii) *rates of change are accelerating.* The rates of ecological change in many parts of the Third World have been insidiously accelerating. The crisis of the Sahel is the outcome of a long decline.[†] The population growth rate in sub-Saharan Africa of over three per cent per annum, with a doubling time of some 23 years, implies unprecedented rates of change in agriculture, livelihoods and social relations; and in other continents too, ecological, economic and social change appear more rapid than before.

(iii) *poor rural people are knowledgeable* (IDS 1979; Brokensha *et al.*, 1980; Richards, 1985). Indigenous technical knowledge (ITK) is now respected more, and valued not only for its validity and usefulness, but because it is part of the power of the poor. ITK is strong on knowledge of local diversity and complexity, precisely where outsiders' knowledge is weak. In rapid change, its advantages over outsiders' knowledge are even greater.

(iv) *rural people are capable of self-reliant organization.* This gross generalization cannot be universal. But that most rural people are more capable of self-reliant organization than most outsiders are conditioned to believe is supported by much evidence (e.g. in Cornell University's *Rural Development Participation Review*).

The *practical* level of the paradigm integrates the other three. A practical approach to development embodies reversals, not just of normal professionalism, but of normal centripetal tendencies. The central thrusts of the paradigm here are decentralization and empowerment. Decentralization means that resources and discretion are devolved, turning back the inward and upward flows of resources and people. Empowerment means that people, especially poorer people, are enabled to take more control over their lives, and secure a better livelihood with ownership and control of productive assets as one key element. Decentralization and empowerment enable local people to exploit the diverse complexities of their own conditions, and to adapt to rapid change. Core programmes spread standardization over diverse realities: the same crops and treatment are recommended in totally different eco-systems; but in the new paradigm, diverse ecological and socio-economic conditions and personal needs generate their own innovations, find their own solutions, and determine their own pathways.

† Author's note (1993). This simple assertion now needs careful qualification.

Decentralization, empowerment, and adaptation to and exploitation of diverse complexity fit and are part of the clearest, most authoritative and most convincing articulation of practical aspects of the new paradigm, by the Kortens and Bagadion (D. Korten, 1980, 1984a and b, 1987; Bagadion and F. Korten, 1985). David Korten has contrasted a blueprint and a learning process approach to development. These correspond closely with normal and new professionalism, except that the new professionalism as advocated in this paper gives more explicit attention to the poorer. Drawing on various D. and F. Korten sources (including personal communications), and with additions, the two paradigms as they apply in approaches to rural development are contrasted in Table 1.2.

Managerially, the blueprint approach fits the type of organization which Burns and Stalker (1961) call mechanistic – with clear and fixed definition of roles, obligations, procedures and methods, hierarchical authority, punitive management style, and inhibited lateral communications. In contrast, the learning process approach corresponds with the type of organization Burns and Stalker call organic – with flexible and changing definitions of

Table 1.2: **The blueprint and learning-process approaches in rural development contrasted**

	Blueprint	Learning Process
idea originates in	capital city	village
first steps	data collection and plan	awareness and action
design	static, by experts	evolving, people involved
supporting organization	existing, or built top down	built bottom-up, with lateral spread
main resources	central funds and technicians	local people and their assets
staff training and development	classroom, didactic	field-based learning through action
implementation	rapid, widespread	gradual, local, at people's pace
management focus	spending budgets, completing projects on time	sustained improvement and performance
content of action	standardized	diverse
communication	vertical: orders down, reports up	lateral: mutual learning and sharing experience
leadership	positional, changing	personal, sustained
evaluation	external, intermittent	internal, continuous
error	buried	embraced
effects	dependency-creating	empowering
associated with	normal professionalism	new professionalism

Source: Adapted from David Korten.

12

roles, obligations, procedures and methods, collegial authority, and free lateral communications. Mechanistic organization is more suited to routine activities in a stable environment, organic to adjusting to a changing environment. The contrast is between a linear, rigid, repetitive machine, and a rounded, flexible, adaptive organism. The learning process and the new paradigm of which it is a part, are not mechanical but evolutionary.

Finally, the new development paradigm is not just a rural Third World phenomenon. It overlaps and resonates with the alternative movements of rich countries (see e.g. Robertson, 1983 and 1985; and Korten and Klauss, 1984). Solutions to the problems of unemployment of the rich world, and of the degraded rotten cores of decaying inner cities, are equally to be sought in decentralization, empowerment, community involvement, and processes of learning. The reversal of learning from, and working collegially with, clients is one of the rediscovered keys to business success (Peters and Waterman, 1982:156–199) as well as an imperative for anti-poverty development.

The practical implications of the new professionalism and the new paradigm can only be sketched here. They have to be worked through and applied to any development situation. Almost always they will challenge what is being done and the way it is being done. Almost always they will meet opposition. But there are now enough examples of successful professional reversals and successful implementation of the new approaches to suggest that they are feasible on a much wider scale.

Conclusion

The new paradigm which I have sketched is primarily derived from and intended for rural development. But it extends to include reversals in international relations, in adverse trends in terms of trade, in the operation of international and bilateral organizations at the macro level, and in policy within both developed and less-developed countries. It concerns professionals who work in the cores as much as those who work in the peripheries.

To what extent the new paradigm can solve the problems which have led development to a crisis depends at one level on changes in professional values, training and rewards. The challenge here is to find 'soft spots', points at which leverage can be exercised. University textbooks, training course materials and syllabi, policies of journal editors, prizes and other forms of recognition for good last-first work – these are some of the options.

At a more immediate level, the paradigm shift depends on professional people. They are the key. The problem is not 'them' (the poor), but 'us' (the not poor). The massive reversals needed to eliminate the worst deprivation need professionals to fight within the structures in which they find themselves. Most, however trapped they feel, have some room for manoeuvre and can find allies. Major shifts come not just from big decisions, though they help, but also gradually through a multitude of small decisions and actions which together build up into a movement. The basic issue is power. Those with power – 'us' – do not easily give it up. The challenge then is to find ways in which more and more of those who are powerful and privileged can be enabled to work to start and strengthen processes which in turn enable and empower those who are weak and deprived.

As I have argued this requires new professionals who, in Herbert Butterfield's phrase, (1949) 'take hold of the other end of the stick', who stand convention on its head, who put people first and poor people first of all.

> Normal professionals face the core
> and turn their backs upon the poor
> New ones by standing on their head
> face the periphery instead.

By doing this they may free themselves from the mental prison of the normal view. With this reversed vision they may see opening up an intellectually exciting agenda of research and, more important, a practically-challenging agenda of action.

To make reversals requires little of a desk-bound academic. It is harder, and takes courage, for those others who combine analysis with engagement in practical affairs. But there are role models, people who have combined excellence in their professional work with a rare and original vision and a commitment to creating institutions to make the world a better place. Fritz Schumacher is one, stigmatised as eccentric, yet influencing all development professions with the message of his three simple words (1973), his writing, and the organization he left behind. Hans Singer is another, at one time branded as 'revolutionary and even subversive' for his prophetic (1950) views on worsening terms of trade for primary producers, yet profoundly influencing development economics with his reversals of view, and policy and practice with his intellectually-creative role in the initiation of UN agencies for development. There have always been new professionals, and when they succeed, as Schumacher and Singer have done, in changing the course of thought and action, it is easy later to underestimate their originality and achievement. Without them, much that we take for granted would not have happened. The question is how to multiply such people.

Whether the new professionalism and the new paradigm can spread and transform the development process on anything like the scale needed cannot be foreseen. But there is less and less reason to doubt that they could. Parallel efforts are needed – conversions of the cores and successes in the peripheries. New professionals, wherever they are, have support from much of the rhetoric of development, but the inertia of the normal has been shifted but little. If the new professionalism and the new paradigm do not become a mainstream in reality, the end of the century may see deprivation more awful in depth and scale even than today. But if they gather momentum and become a movement, there will be hope of major changes for the better. To achieve that momentum and movement is now, as we move towards the twenty-first century, perhaps the greatest challenge facing the development professions.

2 Managing Rural Development: Procedures, Principles and Choices

I've got a little list – I've got a little list
W.S. Gilbert, *The Mikado*

Being the domain of no one discipline or profession, management procedures in rural development have been neglected. East African experiments in the late 1960s and early 1970s suggest useful lessons and principles. These are that analysis and approaches should: be empirical, not perfectionist; use systems thinking; treat administrative capacity as a scarce resource; optimize not maximize; seek optimal ignorance; exploit opportunities, not just tackle problems; and strive for sophistication in simplicity. Procedures are recommended to be participatory, sparing in demands on staff time, and pilot tested. Those who devise and introduce procedures need to have a sound sense of field realities and to share the experience gained. If more professionals launch out and experiment with management procedures, a better sense will be gained of their potential as a means for the poor to gain more.

The main thrust of *Managing Rural Development* is that management procedures are a key point of entry and leverage in securing better performance from government staff in rural development. In the past, procedures have received little attention from those who might have been expected to contribute towards their design, testing and evaluation. They have been neglected by management consultants who are inclined to concentrate on the more prestigious and familiar high-level management in which they are anyway more competent; by central government staff, whether nationals or foreigners – nationals often glad to have escaped from the field and foreigners often ignorant of it; by field staff themselves since they have not been trained in the development of management procedures and are anyway unlikely to be rewarded for innovation; and by academics for whom the safe confines of a discipline are attractive or who lack the time, inclination or access to explore the potential of this largely untouched aspect of rural development. It was only the unusual requirements and opportunities of the Kenya Special Rural Development Programme (SRDP), with its

This chapter draws on experience in Kenya, at a time when the focus was more on procedures for planning and management in Government organizations than for participation by rural people. Since then, approaches and methods for participation by rural people have received more attention and the individual behaviour and attitudes of outsiders have come to be seen as key points of leverage for change. In the 1990s, Government procedures remain important, not least for their influence on officials' behaviour and attitudes and on their interactions with rural people; and in research and development they are still relatively neglected.

15

experimental purpose and its aim of sharpening the machinery of government in rural areas, that drew attention to and encouraged work in this field. This is a realm in rural development which deserves further exploration. To help such exploration this chapter outlines some of the principles and choices thrown up by the experience.

Principles, modes of thought

The principles and precepts which emerge from the experience presented and analysed in *Managing Rural Development* can be described at two levels. The deeper level concerns the modes of thought which underlie statements and prescriptions about management procedures in rural development. Seven principles which are to some extent mutually supporting seem to be particularly important, and are described first. At a second, more operational level, but based on these more general principles, are a number of precepts for procedural design.

The seven modes of thought are:

Empirical not perfectionist
Rural development is complex, is a proper field of study for many disciplines, and is full of variety both within a country and between countries. Rural management is difficult to observe and difficult to manipulate effectively. Complexity and inaccessibility can combine to discourage the researcher, consultant or senior government servant from exposure to the real field situation and conversely to encourage him to fall back on more abstract thought. This can be dangerous. Abstract thought breeds and nourishes perfectionism. It leads away from reality, from what is feasible, and from the cumulative increments of change which can gradually transform performance. It encourages the design and propagation of ideal models which are not only unattainable but also liable to impair rather than improve performance. The perfectionist planner and the intellectual academic are both susceptible to recommending yet more planning – more detailed and specific statement of objectives, the generation and analysis of more data, and the identification and elaboration of more alternatives to choose between. Planning, like politics, is the art of the possible; and perfectionist planning is liable to have two unfortunate effects: generating an insatiable appetite for planners, who are far from costless; and reducing the chances of anything happening on the ground. Exposure to the reality of rural management through accepting responsibility for procedural innovations is a stringent discipline and may even be felt threatening by planners, and more so by academics. Mistakes are made, as I have made mistakes; but the learning process is valuable and should lead to more practical applications than that sort of bad theory which is derived only from the mind without the embarrassment of contact with the confusion of reality. There is here a basic difference of mental set. The development of management procedures can only proceed well if the empirical and not the perfectionist set prevails.

Systems thinking

Although it is not paraded in *Managing Rural Development*, systems thinking is basic to the approach used. This mode of analysis accepts a wide
potential span of relevance, seeks to identify interconnections between
phenomena, and presents simplifications of complex relationships in the
form of diagrams. The clusters of procedures (Figure 2.1) are a simplification of other diagrams which were used at an earlier stage to focus and
clarify discussion and analysis; and while it may seem that this is a simple
outcome, it is doubtful whether this stage would have been reached
without a preceding journey through more complicated diagrams using
systems-thinking techniques. One advantage of this method is the ease with
which shifts in the span of relevance can be accommodated. Thus in drawing boxes and lines connecting them it is always possible to add more so
that additional factors can be taken into account. Given that rural development and rural management are complex both in their nature and in their
potential directions and forms of change, this device is a useful, if not
essential, tool. It has the advantage that at the vital stage of simplification a
wide range of relevant factors can be taken into account in grouping
phenomena. A further benefit is that by identifying the key entities, operations and linkages and presenting these diagrammatically, choices are
more easily seen and listed. In the case of management procedures, Figure
2.1 reveals the choices of where to start as choices between boxes (clusters
of procedures) and lines (linkages between the clusters) or combinations of
these. Without the preceding analysis and this diagram that resulted, these
choices would probably have been less clear. Others who work on rural
management procedures can be expected to come out with different and
more useful categories than these; but they may find it easiest to arrive at
them by using a similar method.

Administrative capacity as a scarce resource

Much of the argument of *Managing Rural Development* is that there are or
could be ways in which the administrative capacity – the capability for
getting things done – of field staff could be substantially increased. It

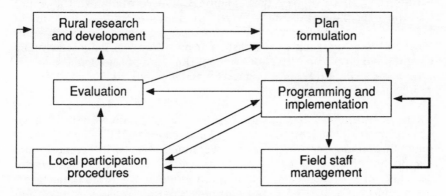

Figure 2.1: *Clusters of procedures and some connections*

17

remains true, though, that the administrative capacity for any operation is finite, that it is a scarce resource, and that consequently it should generally be used sparingly, with preference for activities which are administration-sparing rather than administration-intensive, and for those which make brief rather than persisting demands (Chambers, 1969). There is, however, a widespread tendency, especially in the higher reaches of governments, to fail to recognize the choices implied by this principle and to allow the use of administrative capacity to be unthinkingly preempted by programmes and projects. This may be particularly serious now in the uses made of the limited capability to innovate procedures for rural development; for although the returns to using that scarce capacity may be higher in the rural than in the urban sector, and in recurrent resource management than in capital project management, the choice may be obscured by the urban, capital city, modern and prestigious bias of preferences and activities which, whatever the official pronouncements, influences the behaviour and decisions of many managers, researchers and consultants. The question may be not to what extent scarce centrally-based innovative capacity will be used to increase scarce administrative capacity in the rural areas, but whether it will be so used at all.

Optimizing, not maximizing
The words 'maximize', or 'maximum', or the phrases 'as much as possible' or 'as many as possible' used in connection with rural development and rural management, usually indicate a non-economist author or speaker. Political scientists and sociologists in particular have fallen into a vogue of advocating maximum co-ordination, maximum local participation, involving all groups and all departments at as many levels as possible. This is loose talk and loose thinking. Economists know very well (unless they have been badly trained, or are bad economists) that in complex situations like those of rural development and rural management, in which several scarce resources are involved, multiple objectives are to be satisfied, and multiple outcomes can be anticipated, it is misleading to speak of maximizing any one thing. Maximizing co-ordination or integration would paralyse administration. Maximizing local participation would revolutionize the entire political structure of a country. What is required is a series of informed attempts to optimize a number of resource uses in relation to a number of outcomes, not to maximize any particular one. And this should always be clear if the multiple objectives of rural development policies and the necessarily wide span of relevance in decision making are borne in mind.

Optimal ignorance[1]
There is a profound bias in the Western way of thinking, with its most obvious roots in ancient Greece, that knowledge is good. Applied to the planning and management of rural development this easily promotes and justifies unthinking demands for information – demands which misuse administrative capacity and culminate in mounds of unused data. Information has costs. It is far easier and more natural to ask for, to gather, and to accumulate data, than it is to abstain from asking, to reduce

18

communication, and to limit the information acquired. The challenge here is formidable: it is to reorient thinking radically, to ask not – what do I need to know? Or the more common versions – what would it be interesting to know? What ought I to know in order to be able to defend my conclusions? What have other people asked? What extra can I ask for in order to make my mark? But rather – how much does the information cost? Who is going to process and use it? What benefits will accrue? Will the results be available in time? What can be left out? What simplifications can be introduced? What do we *not* need to know? This moves against the tradition of research, against the bias of the educational system, and against the drives of curiosity, but is in harmony with the principles that administrative (in this case information-gathering) capacity is a scarce resource, and that in complex situations activities should be optimal not maximal. It requires experience and imagination to know what is not worth knowing, and self-discipline and courage to abstain from trying to find it out.

Opportunity- versus problem-orientation
The literature of management and of public administration is frequently concerned with problem-solving and problem-solving capability. The Ndegwa Commission Report in Kenya (Republic of Kenya, 1971a) is a conspicuous example. The paths to development are seen to lead through identifying problems and their causes and then through seeking solutions. It helps here to appreciate that there is an overlap in common usage between the words 'problem' and 'opportunity'. It is possible to present the existence of underdeveloped land in an area as a problem when it might more normally have been regarded as an opportunity.

Notwithstanding this overlap, there are two disadvantages in a problem orientation for rural management. The first is its negative connotations. Problems present themselves; opportunities, however, have to be sought out. The solution of problems is liable to maintain a static situation rather than to promote a developmental one. The attitudes are more those of conservative caretaking government administration than those of an aggressive and enterprising management.

The second disadvantage is that problem-solving may lead to misallocation of resources. If a programme goes badly, solving its problems may involve devoting more resources to it and incurring elsewhere costs quite out of proportion to the benefits from the programme in question. The repeated attempts of the Kenya Department of Agriculture to persuade reluctant (and it need hardly be added – rationally reluctant) farmers to plant cotton is a case in point. The less cotton they grow, the greater the problem and the greater the resources devoted to persuading them to grow more – preempting extension workers' time, convincing farmers that the government is misguided, and demoralizing government staff. An opportunity orientation, by contrast, would have directed attention to a search for crops which would have been more rewarding for the farmers and to seeking out new possibilities in extension rather than concentrating effort on what was already not working.

Sophistication in simplicity
The biases of university education, of intellectual excitement, of desires to extend the boundaries of knowledge, of imagination, of drive and energy – indeed many of the values which are widely accepted as good – are towards complexity. In designing management procedures, the temptation is to introduce more and more requirements and measures, more and more complicated techniques, and more and more elaborate relationships. But such an approach quickly leads to a drop in output and eventually to paralysis. Simplicity has, of course, to be optimal not maximal. To achieve this, ingenuity and courage are needed to devise and use simplifications – though quick and dirty surveys, through collapsing data, through rules of thumb, through the use of proxy indicators – accepting imperfections and inaccuracies as a price it is worth paying in order to improve outcomes; for it is the outcomes which count in evaluation, not the complexities or apparent perfections of the procedures. Given the strong drives towards increasing complexity, a key principle is to be sophisticated in simplicity.

Precepts in procedural design

Besides these general principles some related but more specific and operational injunctions can be culled from East African experience. These may appear rather obvious and common-sense to the reader, but they are so frequently ignored, and I have so often neglected or been in danger of neglecting some of them, that they deserve to be restated and re-emphasized.

Introduce joint programming and joint target-setting
The evidence from the literature on Management by Objectives (Humble, 1969; Garrett and Walker, 1969; Reddin, 1971) and from the SRDP experience is strong that benefits in motivation, timing, anticipation of bottlenecks, and project performance in general can derive from joint programming and joint target-setting. In joint programming, all those directly responsible for implementation should be present and should freely and willingly contribute their ideas and knowledge. In joint target-setting the subordinate should with his supervisor freely take part in drawing up a work programme and agreeing the targets to be achieved. That these two procedures should be innovations is a sad reflection on the underdevelopment of management in the field administrations in Eastern Africa. They require a different style of management to that of the colonial heritage of a quasi-military hierarchy in which decisions are taken at the higher levels and then passed down for execution by junior staff who are required to obey orders and not to reason why. But not only do they require a new style; they help to generate it. The very procedures of joint programming and joint targeting bring together staff whose relationships would otherwise be more distant and more hierarchical, and legitimates and requires a freer form of communication and participation in a common task. In the design of any procedures for rural management a priority should be to identify opportunities to exploit the potential of these techniques.

20

Make meetings few and functional

Meetings have costs: they use staff time and energy. At their worst they lead to frustration and disillusion among the more active attenders, and to a false consensus for poor decisions born of boredom and exhaustion rather than convinced agreement. Meetings should be used sparingly and should be functional. In designing procedures, where meetings are thought to be desirable, the purpose and procedures of the meeting itself should be thought out and specified, together with the expected outcomes and an indication of their usefulness. The costs of meetings in staff time can be reduced by the simple device of starting with those items which are the only concerns of a few people, who can then be released as soon as they have been dealt with. The intervals between meetings can be made longer, as occurred with what were originally monthly management meetings in the SRDP. Or meetings can sometimes be abandoned and a system of *ad hoc* communications or sub-meetings substituted. Meetings can be important, as they are in joint programming and joint target-setting, and where the procedures are clearly laid down and the outputs are functional – directly affecting work to be done.

Make reports short and functional

Most government reporting in rural areas is ritualistic and contains much information that is never used or which, if used, misleads. Application of the principle of optimal ignorance will usually lead to the elimination of items and to shorter reports. Conversely, identification of functions which can best be fulfilled through reports may show new information of a different sort which should be included. The Monthly Management Report in the SRDP is an example of an attempt to design a strictly functional report, which consequently departed from the normal format and normal distribution of reports. Where routine statistical data are required, they should be recorded on standard forms with a clear and simple layout. The costs of any reporting system in terms of staff time and effort should be weighed against the benefits in information *actually used* and any motivational and learning benefits which there may be for the persons reporting.

Subsume or abolish old procedures

New procedures are almost invariably additive: a new item is to be reported, a new return to be sent, a new ledger to be kept, a new committee to be set up; but rarely indeed is the new procedure accompanied by the formal abandonment of the old. Occasionally there is a major convulsion and reports are streamlined, returns and ledgers rationalized, and committees merged or disbanded; but these are the exception not the rule. In introducing new procedures experimentally, it may be necessary at first to add the new system while allowing the old one to continue. But such a situation should not be allowed to persist. Where possible, the new system should subsume the old from the beginning. But whether this will be possible will depend on the degree of access and authority of the person or persons who are introducing the new procedures.

21

Start with a pilot experimental approach

New procedures are usually introduced all at once and then never systematically evaluated. But like any other development initiative, a new procedure should be subject to pilot testing. As with pilot projects generally, there are dangers to be guarded against, including observer effects, unrepresentative conclusions resulting from particular personalities, and other factors peculiar to the experimental situation. A sensible sequence may often be research – design – pilot testing – evaluation – modification – retesting – evaluation and so on, culminating in abandonment or replication. In evaluating new procedures very special care should be taken to allow for unusual behaviour by participants resulting from the experimental situation, particularly if they adopt a deferential attitude towards the researchers. Almost any pilot project can be made to 'succeed' in some sense and researchers must be ready radically to modify or abandon what may work in the experimental situation but which is likely to fail with widespread replication. The experience with the SRDP systems reported in *Managing Rural Development* was that many modifications were necessary in the light of experience, both in the design of forms and in the content of procedures. And it may be noted that at the time of writing, neither of the systems has been replicated.

When replication takes place, a training input may be needed and for this the staff who already know how to operate a management system may be invaluable as trainers. Where a major management system is involved, evaluation should continue after replication. Modifications in different areas or subsequent training inputs may prove necessary.

Involve participating staff in discussing procedures

Participating staff know what they are really doing and this may be quite different from what the designer of the procedures intends or thinks. The literature of organization theory is full of examples of work restriction, of distorted perceptions, of connivance at low performance, or presentation upwards within a hierarchy of information which misleads its recipients. These problems cannot be avoided entirely. But in working out procedures they may be reduced by seeking full and free discussion with those who will use them. The final introduction of the procedures may have to be authoritative; but discussions with participating staff at the design stage and a readiness to modify procedures during testing, are more likely to lead to improvements than to losses.

To end on a note of caution, procedures cannot be a comprehensive panacea. Introduced in isolation, new procedures may be ineffective or harmful, lapsing into bureaucratic ritual or producing unintended results (Molander, 1972). Careful monitoring and supplementary management training are minimal safeguards against these dangers. Another pitfall is excessive administrative innovation leading to signs of a saturation psychosis, described by Laframboise for the Canadian civil service (1971). Procedures may be a key point of entry in attempting to improve performance in rural management; but they are not a complete and sufficient answer to all problems nor a means of exploiting all opportunities. In the short term they may even distract attention from those more conventional concerns – training, terms of service, postings and promotion policies, staff development planning, staff evaluation, work travel facilities, housing, the education of the children of staff – which are properly and understandably the concern of management specialists and of field staff themselves. In the medium term, good procedures will often highlight and provide supporting evidence for the need for longer term reforms in these areas. In the meantime, improved management procedures can be introduced in rural areas more quickly and with an earlier payoff in results.

Choices

If governments are as serious about the priority of rural development as official statements imply, and if the arguments and evidence presented in *Managing Rural Development* are generally accepted, then the design and testing of new management systems and procedures should be a component of any policy which seeks to achieve a more balanced use of manpower resources. This applies in rectifying the overattention paid to urban as against rural development, to plan formulation as against programming and implementation, to capital projects as against recurrent expenditure, and to management training for the centre control headquarters as against the field periphery.

More important, however, the success or failure of new rural management systems and procedures may be central to the question of the extent to which rural equity can be approached through piecemeal social engineering as opposed to utopian and revolutionary solutions. A major issue for the 1970s is whether the behaviour of government field staff can be bent away from those who are already better off and directed much more towards those who are worse off. In this, political will is crucial and can by no means be taken for granted. Without it, isolated innovations and scattered well-meaning attempts by a few civil servants will lead to little. But with it, and with a gathering of experience and skills in this field, it may prove possible to reach many more of those who are being left out and left behind and to help them catch up and benefit more from the changes which are taking place around them. At the very least, determined attempts in these directions seem well worth while.

If this first decision – to give priority to developing management procedures for rural development – is taken, then other choices and decisions follow. The first choice is who should undertake the work and where they should be located. Research and development can be carried out by consultants based in a consultancy organization; by staff from central ministries; by field staff; by the staff of central management units such as the Directorate of Personnel Management in the President's Office in Kenya; by research and teaching staff in institutes of public administration; by university staff from departments of management or of government; or by the staff of research institutes.

There are arguments for and against all of these. Let us consider them in turn. Management consultants may have much relevant expertise but of a rather culture-bound type, and may find it uncongenial (just as governments would find it expensive) if they have to spend a long time in rural areas. Government staff in ministries may have field experience and a good understanding of aspects of the current system, but may take a 'top-down' view of rural management, and may not be available for long enough periods for adequate work. Field staff themselves do quietly innovate in a limited way, but often without a wide awareness of the implications and without relevant training. Staff in central government management units may be best placed for this work if they can be prised away from their desks and from the flow of tenacious demands which prevent them working in rural areas. Staff in institutes of public administration also appear well located for this R and D work, with the added benefit of gaining experience of what actually happens in rural management and the opportunity of using this in their training courses. University teaching staff are another possibility, but they, like central ministry staff, are subject to strong demands on their time, in their case from teaching, examining and the like. Staff working from research institutes may be as well placed as any, particularly if they have a high degree of autonomy in the allocation of their time and lack other pressing commitments. The best policy in any particular country, in the short term at least, is probably to encourage simultaneous initiatives based on a number of different institutions, while keeping communication open between them.

A second choice is what sort of person, with what skills and experience, should be recruited to work on rural management. Wherever possible such people should be nationals whose experience will remain as a national asset. Parts of *Managing Rural Development* are an attempt to make available to others some of the experience Deryke Belshaw and I were priviledged to gain in Kenya. Some foreign contributions may help, but there are dangers here (see also M. Chege, 1973): of the hard sell of the latest trend in management methods; of the culture-bound urban-industrial consultant whose dark suit has never encountered rural mud; of transfers of inappropriate management technology designed for, to paraphrase Nyerere, reaching the moon rather than the village. The most pervasive danger is probably the introduction of excessive paperwork. The mistakes we made should be a warning.

The aim should be to build up a cadre of nationals with experience and expertise in the R and D aspects of rural management. For this the insights of sociology, of organization theory, of management experience, and of agricultural economics appear particularly relevant. We ourselves came to this field from agricultural economics and public administration and found the combination of outlooks useful. But more important than educational and professional backgrounds is a sympathetic understanding of the situation of field staff, a capacity to innovate, and a willingness to work in rural areas. Essential above all is that indefinable sense of what is, and what is not, practicable; and this implies that those with administrative experience may have an advantage over those who have not.

A third complex of choices is where to start. The six clusters of procedures:

- programming, implementation, operational control
- field staff management
- local participation procedures
- evaluation
- rural research and development
- plan formulation

and the linkages between them (see Figure 2.1) make the choices clearer. Our own conclusion is that there will often be higher and quicker benefits from starting with programming, implementation and operational control than with the other clusters, and that the process of developing and diffusing management procedures should be seen as a sequence over time, starting simply and gradually moving into greater complexity as and when it seems desirable. One possibility is to start with an annual programming exercise and then gradually move over the years into action plan formulation tied in with budget procedures.

The choice of where to start will depend, however, on a number of local factors, not least who is available to make the start. If, for example, a capability exists in a department of community development in conjunction with a provincial or regional administration, local participation may appear an appropriate entry. If a ministry of agriculture has adequate central staff, rural research and development may be a relatively easy entry point. The clusters do not, indeed, necessarily have to be linked. There is no overriding reason why initiatives should be connected. Nor is there any reason to regard procedures as a specially difficult field which should not be touched without a mastery of the magic of modern management and systems analysis. Let nothing written here inhibit anyone from trying to improve whatever practices are current. This is a field which no discipline has claimed and which lies open to all. It is one in which common sense, imagination, sensitivity and patience are more important than any formal qualifications. There are many civil servants who are in a position to start at once and exactly where they are, with the practices they use to manage and communicate with their staff and which it is within their discretion to vary. They can begin piecemeal, and without delay. The main thing is to start.

Conclusion

Managing rural development is not a new activity. It is going on all the time. What is perhaps new is treating management procedures for rural development as a field for systematic research and development and suggesting that it should be a concern not only of civil servants but also of others, including university staff. For too long students of public administration have been failing to contribute to national development, to their own frustration and that of their mentors, because of the pre-occupations of the development administration movement (for a critique of which see Schaffer, 1969) and because of the wide gap between researchers and the actual detailed, mundane but vital processes and procedures by which

25

government bureaucracies operate. I hope that *Managing Rural Development* will help to show that this futility need not persist; that there is an opportunity for useful work; that those whose field of study is public administration can, as has already been done in Kenya (Chabala *et al.*, 1973), examine procedures, comment upon them and their effects, and suggest modifications. The only valid excuse for public administration academics who complain that their work is not useful to governments should be that they lack access. Lack of professional competence is scarcely an excuse in an activity which is as uncharted as this. Competence is gained by doing, by plunging in and gathering experience on the run while bringing to bear those wider perspectives of which university staff should pre-eminently be aware. There emerges a strong argument, therefore, for departments of government or public administration in universities shifting focus to include research and development in rural management procedures. This would, as again already in Kenya, have the added advantage of gradually creating a national resource of former students with experience, skills and insight in this field.

Taking a wider view, what matters is that more people, whether civil servants, university staff, students or others, should be concerned with procedures for rural management, that more new approaches should be tried, and above all that the findings should be written up and become part of the stock of public and international knowledge. There are powerful reasons for the exchanges of knowledge and insight being direct between the countries where rural development is a priority. But first that knowledge and insight must be made explicit. There is already a wealth of experience locked up in the minds and memories of civil servants but which they have hitherto rarely analysed or presented. Procedures have tended to be regarded by them as well as by researchers as a rather dull part of the job, not worth much attention, and certainly not worth writing about. If *Managing Rural Development* has begun to show that to the contrary they are an exciting field for innovation, that they are worth writing about, that there is value in sharing experience, it will have served much of its purpose.

If rural management becomes a major concern, then the evidence and arguments presented here will be seen as preliminary, partial and fumbling. No doubt some of the conclusions will turn out to be premature; no doubt some of the generalizations will prove to be wrong. But the purpose has been to try to open up the subject and present possible starting points for others. As with research and development work generally, it is not easy to forecast with any accuracy the potential of this field of activity. It may be great. What we need, and need quickly, is a clearer appreciation of the extent of that potential. This will only be possible if others launch out into this challenging and exciting area. If they do not, a major chance may be missed. If they do, perhaps they will discover much more effective techniques which can be used for making life better for those, particularly those who are worse off, who live and will continue to live in the rural areas of the third world.

3 Project Selection for Poverty-focused Rural Development: Simple is Optimal

> If we could turn official and popular interest away from the grandiose projects and to the real needs of the poor, the battle could be won.
>
> E.F. Schumacher, *Small is Beautiful*

Many obstacles face the selection of effectively poverty-focused rural projects. Poor rural people are hard to reach. The small projects often required may conflict with donor and political needs for big projects. The complex appraisal procedures of social cost-benefit analysis obscure the basis for decisions, are in practice abused, and both neglect and pre-empt scarce administrative capacity. They can lead to dependence, delays and pressures to spend. They can bias project selection away from the poorer rural people and the poorer countries.

Selection can be improved through decentralizing project selection, presenting information clearly for decisionmaking, improving the judgement of decisionmakers through direct rural exposure, and inventing and adopting procedures based on the principle that simple is optimal.

Introduction

This chapter takes as its point of departure the rhetoric of donor agencies and of national plans, which requires a high priority for rural development, and especially for rural development that will benefit the poorer people. It is concerned with project selection, both in theory and in practice. It takes project selection to include identification, design, appraisal and choice. It does not tackle issues of radical redistribution, for example through land reform, vital though that sometimes is as a precondition for major help to poorer rural people; nor does it consider vital questions concerning the political organization of poor people. It is confined to projects which are selected by donors, governments and other agencies, and which might be considered suitable for formal appraisal procedures.

A problem in thinking constructively about project selection for poverty-focused rural development is the temptation to start with appraisal methodology. The corpus of literature on social cost-benefit analysis is large, accessible, and, despite its critics, invested with an aura of sophistication and authority. If, however, our objective is to improve project selection so as to reduce rural poverty, then the right starting point is not the means but the end, not the library but the village, not the methodology of appraisal but the poorer rural people. Starting from them rather than from the cost-benefit paradigm, and trying to see what approaches will help them rather than consummate the training in project appraisal which many economists have received, leads away from complex procedures and towards the conclusion that for these purposes true sophistication lies in simplicity: in short, that simple is optimal.

Rural poverty: problems and opportunities

The poorer rural people are hard to reach. They are typically unorganized, inarticulate, often sick, seasonally hungry, and quite frequently dependent on local patrons. They are less educated, less in contact with communications, less likely to use government services, and less likely to visit outside their home areas than their better-off rural neighbours. They are often especially concentrated in regions remote from urban centres. Further, they are relatively invisible, especially the women and children. Urban-based officials and foreign experts alike can easily, as 'rural development tourists', make rural visits without either seeing or speaking to the poorer people. Residentially, they are often separate. A week could be spent in South India visiting villages without ever entering one of the harijan colonies where many of the very poorest live. In parts of Africa, roadside elites are emerging as the richer people buy up the more desirable plots beside the roads and build good houses there, while the poorer people increasingly shift away out of sight.[1] Visitors tend to see, to meet, and to interact with, only the more influential and better off rural people.

As though these were not obstacles enough, there is the notorious tendency – the 'talents effect' (Pearse, 1977) – for the rich to get richer and the poor to remain as they are or to get poorer. Projects and programmes for rural development are again and again captured by rural elites for their own advantage. Credit goes to the creditworthy who are those who least need it. Subsidized inputs supplied through a co-operative are monopolised by the leaders of the co-operative who are the better-off people to start with. There seems to be a general law that the greater the amount of money that has to be spent in a rural development programme and the shorter the period in which that money has to be spent, the more likely it is that the rural elite will benefit disproportionately.

The selection of poverty-focused projects has to take account of these realities. Developments which generate livelihoods, which create new demands for rural labour, which provide services to which all have effective access, or which enable poor people to support one another and to organize themselves in groups, will usually be preferred in a poverty-focused approach. Some large projects which distribute or redistribute productive assets to poor people (including some irrigation and settlement projects) may score well. But many of the most effective initiatives will look very different from traditional large high-capital projects. They may emphasize institutions. They may seek to combine experiment with replicability. They may involve, for example, forms of agricultural organization for small farmers, or for landless labourers, or for women; or procedures for recruiting smaller farmers for farmer training courses; or the development of alternative sources of income for landless agricultural labourers in the off-season; or improvements in the management of irrigation bureaucracies; or the provision of mobile services for nomadic people. For these and similar initiatives, local-level institutions and procedures have a central importance.

In future it seems that many of the most effective poverty-oriented rural projects will in practice be:

(i) small. Even where a programme may be quite large, for example for building rural health posts, its component projects may be small;
(ii) administration-intensive rather than capital- or import-intensive. The amount of administrative input per dollar expended will be high;
(iii) difficult to monitor and inspect. Many of the most effective programmes will be highly dispersed, and will often involve actions like the formation of groups or the construction of small items of infrastructure which are not easy to inspect;
(iv) slow to implement.[2] Dispersed construction faces logistic problems; scattered staff are difficult to supervise; remote areas are difficult to reach; local participation (so widely advocated but so rarely analysed) implies going at the people's pace; poor people often take time to realise what they can achieve and there are many obstacles to their becoming organized;
(v) not suitable for complex techniques for project appraisal. Geographical dispersal, uncertainties about implementation, low project costs, and the large numbers of projects combine to make standard complex techniques for project appraisal both expensive and inappropriate.

If this is where many of the needs and opportunities lie, much of the aid and investment process appears still to point in other directions. A gap yawns between the rhetoric of poverty-orientation and the realities of resource allocation and effective access to resources. Project selection is only one part of that gap. Its importance, and the justification for considering it here, is that it is a part of the process where many crucial decisions are taken or pre-empted, and where much analysis and intervention are concentrated. To understand how it might be improved we must examine some of the obstacles to effective poverty-orientation on the part of governments and, more especially, of donors.

Problems in project selection

The problems discussed below are by no means a complete list; but they do comprise some of the more serious difficulties in effective selection for poverty-focused projects.

The needs of donors
In contrast with the rural poor, the rich donors are well-organized, articulate, educated, concentrated in urban centres, and above all, powerful. Their needs are many and various. They include a need to satisfy themselves that their funds are being 'well-spent', as well as a need actually to spend them. The poverty-orientation of many donors in recent years has made it harder to find suitable projects. There is a common lament that poverty-oriented projects are

scarce. Donors compete with one another to aid a few favourite poverty-oriented countries, and in other countries to support the few poverty-oriented projects which can be found. But as the need to spend persists and even becomes more acute and as their expenditures come under critical scrutiny donors are still impelled to prefer projects which is practice are:

- large;
- capital- and import-intensive rather than administration-intensive;
- easy to monitor and inspect;
- quick to implement (using foreign skills where necessary); and
- suitable for social cost-benefit analysis.

These preferences are reinforced by some of the writing about development. Analysts of development have tended to pay more attention to large than to small projects. Large projects are more familiar to economists from industrial countries; funds, at least in the past, may have been more readily available to study them than to study small projects; data from them may have been more accessible; and they have lent themselves to conventional methods of *ex ante* appraisal and *ex post* evaluation. Thus 28 out of the 29 projects analysed in King's *Economic Development Projects and Their Appraisal* (1967) were for major infrastructure; and although his analysis was far from conventional, Hirschman's eleven cases in *Development Projects Observed* (1967) were all large-scale. Roads, power, multi-purpose valley development, industries like cement, paper and steel, and large agricultural or irrigation projects, have tended to be the most visible, the most prestigious, the most visited and the most written about. More recent studies, such as Uma Lele's *The Design of Rural Development: Lessons from Africa* (1975), although still examining some large projects, have shifted attention towards smaller, more scattered and decentralized initiatives to reach and help the rural poor. The question is to what extent can and will donors and recipient governments similarly shift their sights and priorities.

The big project trap
The shift is difficult because interlocking forces bias donors and recipient governments alike towards large projects. The reasons are commonplace. For some donors, big is beautiful because big is bankable; pressures to spend aid funds are best overcome through large projects, often for infrastructure. Such projects tend to have a high import content, which pleases industrialized donors. They are usually highly visible and photogenic which pleases political leaders and civil servants alike. They are professionally challenging. They may provide opportunities for corruption at the higher levels of government. They provide contacts for local professionals and civil servants which may make it easier for them to join the brain drain to the richer world. Consultant firms throughout the world find large projects a source of profitable employment. Implementation can be assured where necessary though the use of foreign skills. Finally the methods of appraisal for such projects have been quite highly developed, routinized and accepted and have a measure of general utility.

Because of the conjuncture of all these factors, big projects can be a trap.

30

Moreover, the trap may close much earlier than is commonly realised. Irreversibility of commitment, whether by recipient or donor, whether by politician or civil servant, does not feature much if at all in the literature of project appraisal. But the 'yes-no' decision about a project begins to close and often closes before any formal cost-benefit appraisal can be carried out. Cost-benefit approaches may then be useful in the design stage in improving choices between alternative designs, but they will have become irrelevant to the decision to invest which, in terms of political realities, has already been taken.

To the extent that big projects are needed to support or complement poverty-oriented programmes, or to the extent that, as with some agricultural settlement and irrigation projects, they are directly poverty-oriented, it may not matter unduly in itself that they represent the needs of donors and of governments, and that they trap them at an early stage.

But there is a recurrent danger that a big project will divert resources (including administrative resources) and attention away from other better projects or activities. An example is the Tarbela dam in Pakistan which is expected to cost $1.2 billion. It has been estimated that the water it will make available to irrigators will be less than one-third of what might be saved for a fraction of the cost through improved management of existing irrigation in Pakistan.[3] This appears to be a case where a highly visible and prestigious project has focused attention in the wrong place, away from less spectacular but much more rewarding opportunities. More generally, big projects may provide diversions which make it easier to avoid grasping the nettle of rural poverty. In the 1960s some large projects were described as white elephants which became sacred cows. With the poverty-orientation of the 1970s, some are red herrings.

Project appraisal in practice
A further possible obstacle to effective poverty-oriented projects is the tendency towards complexity and obscurity in methods of appraisal. Whatever has happened to the economies of the poor countries, the literature of project appraisal has an impressive record of growth. The observer may be forgiven for wondering where it will all end, as some try to develop appraisal methods which will keep pace with changing criteria of appraisal (new criteria being added rather than old ones being subtracted) and practitioners struggle to follow their advice. One question here is whether the addition of employment and poverty criteria to social cost-benefit analysis will lead to a net improvement in resource allocation. To answer this question would require a major study. A positive case can be argued at both theoretical and practical levels. Certainly, in practice, the questions asked of a project during appraisal can influence the 'yes-no' decision, and also design. The negative case, however, often goes by default because it does not fit into the cost-benefit paradigm. In presenting parts of the negative case, the purpose here is to raise issues of concern rather than to pretend to definitive answers.

Any evaluation of a method of project appraisal should be based not on its appearance, nor on the theory of how it should be applied, but on what happens in practice. It is not the study of manuals and procedures that is relevant but the study of behaviour. Analyses from the standpoint of public administration and political science, like those of Caiden and Wildavsky (1974) and Self (1975) are valuable not least because they admit forms of evidence about behaviour which some mathematicians and some economists might be inclined to disregard or discount. In the writer's experience it is common to find that practitioners of social cost-benefit analysis admit in private that what appears as a clinical and objective procedure is in practice a compound of judgement about future events which are very difficult to predict, and judgement about discount rates and shadow prices within limits which allow for wide variation. The uncertainties and difficulties are especially acute with agricultural projects. In one case reported to the writer the same agricultural project appraised by three different teams was accorded rates of return of 19 per cent, 13 per cent and minus 2 per cent, respectively, much of the variation being explicable in terms of differing estimates of rates of implementation and/or the adoption of innovations, both of which are inherently difficult to anticipate.

It may be asked to what extent the combination of uncertain judgement and methodological complexity exposes social cost-benefit analysis to political pressures. Ironically, appraisal techniques developed to make decision-making more rational may be used to legitimize decisions, arrived at in other ways. Partly this is possible because of the obscurity of the calculations when final data are presented to a decisionmaker. Partly it may occur because decisionmakers know that the results are easily manipulable. Far from defending appraisers from political pressures, the procedures may then expose them all the more. In practice, rates of return are sometimes determined first and the calculations done later to produce them; and there are more subtle personal and political interactions between calculations and desired results.[4] The danger is that the addition of employment and poverty criteria to social cost-benefit analysis will have little effect because the procedure itself is so sensitive to judgement and so vulnerable to personal factors and to political pressure.

Complexity, dependence and delay

Complex procedures may also contribute to and sustain dependence and delay. The combination of pressure to find projects, shortage of good projects, and the demand of donors for complex appraisals, creates congestion. The response of many international agencies is to intervene in project preparation. But as Rondinelli (1976a) has argued in an examination of the World Bank, USAID and UNDP.

The direct intervention of international agencies in project preparation is in part a response to the severe deficiencies in planning and project analysis skills in developing nations, but the 'deficiencies' are in a sense, artificially created by the complexity of international procedures. Project preparation guidelines are designed to ensure that proposals are compatible with lending institution policies, procedures and requirements; and as such have become instruments of control rather than of aid. And as those procedures become more numerous and complex, further de-

32

mands are placed on the limited planning and administrative capacity of developing nations, making them more dependent on foreign expertise . . . the imposition of international requirements . . . may in fact, have aggravated the problem of preparing relevant and appropriate investment proposals (p.3)

The argument of this chapter is not that there are no benefits from such procedures. The question is to what extent the costs of following the procedures are justified by the benefits. For the costs can be high, especially in the poorest countries which are precisely those in which the procedures are most difficult to carry out. Donors are liable to respond to these difficulties in ways which either sustain dependence (by posting in their own staff to do the job) or which reduce benefits to the poorer people within countries, or by concentrating on other countries. To quote Rondinelli (1976a) again:

The limited staff time within aid agency headquarters leads to a preference for large projects in developing countries with better project preparation capabilities or with access to technical consultants, than for smaller projects in poorer countries with limited preparation capabilities (p.20).

There may thus be a syndrome in which what passes for sophistication in project selection actually hinders aid to the poorest. Donors bring to bear 'an imperious rationality' (Rondinelli, 1976b) on recipients. The laborious procedures required delay projects. Delays to projects increase pressures for donors to spend. Pressures to spend exert biases towards the less poor developing countries, towards larger projects, towards urban areas (Lipton, 1977), towards the more accessible rural areas, and, within rural areas, towards those who are better off. In short, complex procedures can divert development efforts away from the poorer rural people.

The neglect of administrative capacity
Again and again administrative capacity – the capacity to get things done – emerges as a preoccupation. It is, indeed, often the most critically scarce resource (see also pp. 17–18). Problems of implementation, above all in the rural sector, are an almost universal lament. Lele (1975:176) concluded from her study of rural projects in Africa that the most important factor in limited effectiveness was the 'extreme scarcity of trained local manpower'. The shortage of good rural projects is often a crippling impediment. The capacity to spend is often severely limited. In Botswana, in the three years from 1973/74 to 1975/76, the Ministry of Agriculture was able to spend only 30 per cent of its development budget. The capacity to implement is often a far, far scarcer resource limiting achievement than any other factor; but the implications of this fact have apparently not been incorporated in procedures for project appraisal.

Three aspects of the scarcity of administrative capacity deserve attention. First, managerial and technical skills attracted to a project may have a high cost in terms of benefits foregone elsewhere in the economy. The ODA Manual has a significant line. 'The supreme importance of good management for the success of a project must always be kept in mind'

33

(ODA, 1972:23). The recurrent danger is that donors will insist on recruiting high-level nationals to manage projects, removing them from key posts of greater importance. This cost does not feature in the Manual by Little and Mirrlees (1974) who list land, labour, capital, foreign exchange and savings among their scarce resources, but not administrative capacity. The nearest they come to considering it is in the shadow pricing of skilled labour (ibid. 229–31). They write 'If there is a shortage of skilled people (and for many categories of skills this is true and likely to remain true for some time in the case of many developing countries) then . . . one cannot do better than ask what employers are willing to pay for the relevant skills'. The accounting price would then be the price which would eliminate any excess demand for such skills. And they conclude that 'it does not seem to us that very much time should normally be spent on contemplating the problems raised in this section'. But especially in countries where managerial or technical talent is scarce, the costs to the economy of the removal from their posts of key nationals to work on a new project may be very high indeed, and grossly underestimated by costing at the price which would eliminate any excess demand for their skills. Thus the true cost of a project may be seriously underestimated by neglecting administrative capacity as a scarce resource. More specifically for our purposes, the unasked question is whether the managerial and technical staff recruited to a project will be brought from posts and activities in which they would have made a greater contribution to alleviating rural poverty.

Second, administrative capacity in existing organizations is inelastic. A government organization used for one programme may not be able simultaneously to carry out another. Demands for information can have high costs in other field staff activities foregone. The introduction of a programme for agricultural credit to be implemented by an extension agency may appear desirable, but any be anti-developmental because of other extension activities which it crushes or pre-empts. In Mwanza District in Tanzania, the arrival of tractors diverted agricultural extension staff from a promising programme for improving cotton production among the generality of farmers to a narrow programme of mechanization. Not only was the mechanization a failure, but the high potential benefits of the extension programme were lost (Chambers, 1969). This point has a strong bearing on the poverty orientation. Since much poverty-oriented rural development is administration-intensive, special care has to be taken in the allocation of field staff time between alternative activities. Unless this is done, programmes may be introduced which appear beneficial but the net effect of which is to reduce the impact of government action on rural poverty.

Third, the time of economists and planners is itself a scarce resource. Cost-benefit analysis has costs and benefits itself. But a survey of some of the texts on project appraisal (McKean, 1965; King, 1967; Harberger, 1972; ODA, 1972; OECD, 1972; Little and Mirrlees, 1974; Squire and van der Tak, 1975; Irvin, 1976; Bergmann and Boussard, 1976; and Scott, MacArthur and Newbery, 1976) reveals that they concentrate almost exclusively on procedures of analysis and their presumed benefits while ignoring or not considering in any detail the costs of carrying them out.[5]

34

Whether some economists have a mental block, or a becoming if uncharacteristic modesty, when it comes to costing their scarce selves may be a whimsical speculation. But only when their time is treated as a scarce resource can good decisions be made about optimal levels of complexity in project selection. An exception is provided by Carruthers and Clayton who do evaluate project appraisal from the point of view of the demands it makes on skilled effort. They write that

> . . . the laborious process of shadow pricing, according to the manuals, absorbs an undue amount of skilled effort while *ex post* evaluation reveals that the factors which determine project success or failure are not primarily related to these aspects of planning (1977:9–10).

The point is important since poverty-oriented rural development is likely to require the processing of more small projects. Appraisal procedures should not only be relevant; they should also be sparing in their demands on the time of skilled manpower. If they are not sparing, the danger is that appraisal bottlenecks will reduce the net contribution of projects in alleviating rural poverty and will divert economists and planners from more crucial tasks.

Solutions: simple is optimal

General prescriptions follow from this discussion. Biases based on the needs of donors and sustained by some past writing on development should be consciously offset. Big projects should be approached with circumspection. Data requirements for appraisal should be restrained. The considerations on which decisions are to be based should be clear to decisionmakers. The costs of complex procedures should be recognized. Administrative capacity, including the time of economists and planners, should be treated as a scarce resource. Taken together, these prescriptions imply that for the many rather small projects which are essential in any poverty-orientation, methods of selection are needed which are simple, open to inspection, and readily intelligible, and which either make sparing demands on scarce skills or concentrate their demands on skills, which are underused. Furthermore, steps should be taken to improve the judgements inevitably involved in selection.

Three approaches are suggested to satisfy these requirements. They have in common a thrust towards simplicity – in decentralized administration, in appraisal procedures, and in the life styles and experience of officials.

Decentralization

Poverty-focused rural development requires changes of direction and emphasis. It is true that major infrastructure in the form of roads and other communications, storage facilities, and the like are often a necessary precondition for or complement to smaller projects. But for the reasons presented above, large projects have been given high priority, and much more attention has now to be given to smaller, lower-level initiatives. The sheer volume of identification and appraisal work that these could entail could easily overwhelm central government and aid agency officials. There is already a sad history of district-level planning in some countries and regions (such as Kenya, Tanzania and Zambia for their second Five-Year Plans, and Tamil Nadu in 1973/4) in which many projects have been worked out in the districts and submitted in long heterogeneous shopping lists to the centre, only to be ignored because of the poor quality of the submissions and the impossibility of handling so much detail. The results have been disillusion among field staff, political embarrassment at all levels, and high stacks of mouldering documents gathering dust on the shelves of offices. For the future, the only way forward on any scale appears to be through effective decentralization.

For such decentralization to work, financial discretion has to be given to staff at the local level. One pattern which may deserve serious trials where it does not yet occur is a block grant system in which each financial year a sum of money is made available to local-level officials to spend at their discretion on projects which accord with centrally-determined guidelines. These guidelines can stipulate that the main beneficiaries of projects should be poorer rural people. Experience with block grants has already been gained in East Africa (Collins, 1974; Chambers, 1974:94–100). There are, of course, dangers of misallocations and of corruption. Cautious accountants and auditors often distrust local-level officials; but the distrust becomes self-validating when those officials are given little discretion and thus little opportunity to demonstrate their capabilities. In many countries, field staff constitute a major, very expensive, and underused resource. Only by giving them more discretion and resources can they realise their potential. Donors who do not have a local cost constraint are particularly well-placed for this sort of assistance.

With decentralization combined with central guidelines, the administration-intensive processes of identification and preparation can be undertaken by the often underused local-level staff. Central government staff, including planners and economists, can have monitoring and training roles which are much less exacting than carrying out identification and appraisal themselves. And many more small initiatives can be undertaken to the benefit of the rural poor.

Simple procedures
An essential part of any poverty-focused rural development is the devising and use of simple procedures. There is an almost universal tendency for procedural overkill. Procedures are almost always additive: new ones are introduced, but old ones are not abolished. Procedures drawn up by committees, or through consultation with various people or departments, tend to be longer and more complicated that those drawn up by one person – and participative management may reinforce this tendency. It is often safer to add a requirement for an additional item of information than to leave it out. Promotions go to bright people who can devise and answer questions, and not to those who tell their superiors that they do not consider the benefits of being able to answer their questions justify the costs of collecting the information necessary.

36

A first step is then to have the insight to see what it is not worth knowing, and the courage not to find it out. Courage is needed because optimal simplicity looks naive.

Simple procedures are also necessary if decisions are to be kept in the open, making it clear to the decision-maker what criteria are being used, and how the method works. As Carruthers (1977) has commented in reviewing Squire's and van der Tak's *Economic Analysis of Projects*, 'A practice has not much to recommend it if the working of the method and the decision criteria are not evident to the decision-makers'. As we have noted, the obscurity of some social cost-benefit analysis exposes it to abuse. It is easy, and known to be easy, to adjust assumptions (discount rates, shadow prices, rates of implementation or adoption, etc.) to produce a wide range of results. Rationality may be defended through selection procedures in which the assumptions are always clear and which so far as possible can be understood by a non-economist decision-maker.

Five simple approaches are suggested. Probably none is new. Most or all of them may be used in governments and aid agencies already, especially for small projects. But curiously, while social cost-benefit manuals are published and widely distributed, these simpler aids to selection are rarely written about. They should be the subject of much more serious comparative study.

Decision matrices   As argued by Carruthers and Clayton (1977), decision matrices can be used to present alternatives clearly, keeping factors separate instead of conflating them into a single numeraire. They enable the decisionmaker to assign his/her own implicit weights and to understand more clearly the implications of his decisions. They can be used to present the implications for the poorer people of alternative projects or alternative approaches to the same project.

Poverty group ranking   Poverty group rankings are a device for concentrating thought and attention on which groups in the society will benefit from a project. They require those preparing a project to ask the crucial 'who benefits?' question, and to rank groups according to their degree of benefit. The question should make low administrative demands on those who have to answer them. The result should be to force officials, whether in ministries or in decentralized administrations, to think at an early stage about beneficiaries; and the procedure can be designed so that those originating a proposal for a project have to defend the rankings which they have given it. Such a system should benefit the poorer rural people by affecting the thinking, behaviour and choices of those who identify, design and select projects.

Checklists   Checklists of factors to consider are widely used but little written about (but see ODA, 1972 and Government Affairs Institute, 1976:15–29). They may be used specifically to alert appraisers to considerations such as poverty, employment and administrative capacity. Some officials have their own checklists. Checklists do, however, run the risk of becoming too long. As with other procedures it is optimal to stay simple.

Listing costs and benefits Where some sort of cost-benefit appraisal is needed for a small project, a simple approach is to list anticipated costs and benefits putting figures on them as appropriate. This approach is illustrated in the OXFAM *Field Directors' Handbook* (1976, Section 5), and also put forward by the Government Affairs Institute in their book, *Managing Planned Agricultural Development* (1976), which recommends identifying 'all relevant aspects of proposed projects, quantifying those costs and benefits for which data are available, and to which monetary values can be assigned without violating common sense' (p.29). While the word 'all' is dangerous, since with ingenuity one can add almost endlessly to minor externalities, the approach in practice is likely to be intelligible and to provide a potential basis for reasonable decisions.

Unit costs and cost-effectiveness Unit cost and cost-effectiveness criteria are widely applicable and useful. They are used by OXFAM, with rules of thumb for different types of project, and an 'index of unit costs' which is the cost of a project divided by the number of people benefiting. They are especially useful with projects for health, education, water supply and the provision of other services.

These five procedures are open to criticism by perfectionists. The traditions and methods of mathematics value precision. But in practical decisionmaking there are optimal levels of imprecision and ignorance. The key to optimizing procedures is to realise that the cost-effectiveness of the procedures themselves relates to low costs in staff time and in demands for information as against high benefits in improving the quality of the decisions. The danger is that 'intelligent' criticism of simple procedures will consider only the benefit side and neglect the costs, leading to 'improvements' which make the procedures more laborious, less practical, more costly to carry out, and counter-productive. Complexity and sophistication are not synonymous; on the contrary, complexity can be crude and naive. The true sophistication is to see how far it is optimal to be simple.

Life-styles, learning and judgement
A danger remains that demands for information by bilateral and multilateral donors will develop a galloping elephantiasis which will paralyse administrations, reduce aid to the poorest, and perpetuate and increase dependence on foreign expertise. The danger is that more and more highly trained and experienced people will be sucked or enticed into the prestigious, well-paid, urban-biased business of project identification, appraisal, monitoring and evaluation. Thus at a time when rural development has become a priority, especially the much more difficult objective of rural development which benefits the poorer rural people, there may perversely be less and less contact between those responsible for rural projects and policies on the one hand and poor rural people on the other. These trends can be moderated by the decentralization and the simple procedures advocated above. But there is one more measure to be taken: a conscious and determined drive to counteract the effects of the urban and elite life-styles,

38

experiences and perceptions of many of those concerned with rural policies and programmes. The seriousness of the need varies by country and region. But the reform proposed is a requirement by every donor agency, and selectively by governments, that their officials should be systematically exposed and encouraged to learn about rural life and especially rural poverty. This could mean, for donors, that each official would be required to spend two weeks of every year actually living in a village,[6] not making the easier, more congenial visits of a rural development tourist, thereby learning how rural people, and especially the poor rural people, live, and so trying better to understand their needs.

The benefits would be many. Some officials would resign. Others would work harder and better. The asymmetry of the aid relationship would be mitigated, since 'donors' would have to go cap-in-hand to 'recipients' and ask them to allow their 'donor' staff to be recipients of experience in the villages.

The main benefit would be improved judgement. However carefully procedures are devised, training undertaken, and feasibility appraised, the element of judgement always has a major part to play in project selection. With poverty-focused rural development, judgement must be based upon an understanding of rural realities. Direct exposure to village life, if sensitively managed, should enable officials better to assess rural needs, better to appreciate the capabilities of rural people and their potential for participation, and better to understand and counteract the tendency for projects to be captured by rural elites. Officials should become better judges of implementability and of rates of change. They might repeatedly learn and relearn the lesson that simple is optimal. The outcome should, indeed, be that more projects would be selected and implemented which would truly benefit the poorer rural people in ways which they would welcome.

4 Health, Agriculture, and Rural Poverty – Why Seasons Matter

I say to the father of my child, 'Father of Podi Sinho,' I say, 'There is no *kurakkan* in the house, there is no millet and no pumpkin, not even a pinch of salt. Three days now and I have eaten nothing but jungle leaves. There is no milk in my breasts for the child.' Then I get foul words and blows. 'Does the rain come in August?' He says. 'Can I make the *kurakkan* flower in July? Hold your tongue, you fool. August is the month in which the children die. What can I do?'   *The Village in the Jungle* by Leonard Woolf[1]

This chapter argues that in many tropical environments the wet season is the most critical time of year, especially for the poorer people, women and children. Commonly at that time malnutrition, morbidity and mortality peak; the costs of sickness – to society in lost agricultural production, and to families in food and income foregone – are at their highest; sickness is most liable to make poor people permanently poorer; and health services are likely to be at their least effective. But systematic biases prevent urban-based professionals from adequately perceiving this seasonal deprivation; they tend to underestimate morbidity in wet seasons and not to recognise its social and agricultural impacts. More needs to be know about impoverishment through seasonal sickness, about micro-level seasonal linkages, and about zones of adverse seasonalities; and priority is indicated for research on tropical diseases with seasonal impacts on agriculture. More immediately, seasonal analysis has practical implications for the management of health services, including the supply of medicaments, preventive and curative measures, crèches for working mothers, and the selection of community health workers able to provide care at the times of greatest need. Finally, decentralized seasonal analysis is proposed. This would bring rural health and agricultural staff together to identify local linkages between health, nutrition, agriculture and poverty, and then to plan and implement programmes geared to the seasonal needs of the poorer and more vulnerable people.

The argument

This chapter[2] argues that in many tropical rural environments the wet season is the most difficult and critical time of year, especially for the poorer people, women, and children. The 'wet season' here refers to the period from the onset of rains until the harvest. This wet season is often the time when morbidity and mortality are highest, when people are most incapacitated by sickness, when rural health services are least likely to be effective, and when urban-based officials are least likely to observe what is happening in rural

40

areas. The seasonal dimension is important in determining medical research priorities, and in planning and administering preventive and curative health programmes. Seasonal analysis presents an opportunity for improving health care at the times when it is most needed.

The main argument is presented in the form of seven propositions:

- most of the very poor people in the world live in rural tropical environments of marked wet-dry seasonality;
- malnutrition, morbidity and mortality have seasonal patterns and often peak during the wet season;
- the poorer people, women and children are especially vulnerable to hardship, malnutrition, sickness and death in the wet season;
- the economic costs of sickness and weakness are concentrated in the wet season;
- it is during the wet season that sickness is most liable to make people permanently poorer;
- rural health services are likely to be at their least effective in the wet season;
- urban-based professionals underperceive seasonal deprivation and underestimate morbidity in the wet season.

The seven statements will be discussed in turn. They are not generalizations with universal validity. The critical reader will recognise that there are exceptions to most, if not all, of them. Environments vary and each should be examined separately. Nevertheless, the evidence so far assembled (see Chambers, Longhurst and Pacey, 1981) suggests a seasonal scenario in which many factors are adverse during and just after the rains. In this scenario,

for agriculturalists in the tropics, the worst times of year are the wet seasons, typically marked by a concurrence of food shortages, high demands for agricultural work, high exposure to infection especially diarrhoeas, malaria and skin diseases, loss of body weight, low birth weights, high neo-natal mortality, poor child care, malnutrition, sickness and indebtedness. In this season, poor and weak people, especially women, are vulnerable to deprivation and to becoming poorer and weaker. (Chambers *et al.*, 1979, summary, and see pp.158–60 for an extended version of the scenario)

Most of the very poor people in the world live in rural tropical environments of marked wet-dry seasonality   Climatic seasonality in the tropics has been defined and measured in several different ways (Walsh, 1981). One distinction is between unimodal (single peak) and bimodal (double peak) patterns of rainfall, with their associated patterns of agriculture. Another approach, developed by Walsh (ibid.) distinguishes relative seasonality (degree of contrast between the rainfall of different times of the year) and absolute seasonality (length of the dry period). Using Walsh's classification system to eliminate areas like Kerala and the Congo basin which have low relative and absolute seasonalities, the rural populations subject to marked climatic

41

seasonality in Africa south of the Sahara have been estimated at about 220 million and in the Indian subcontinent at about 600 million (Chambers, 1981). With the addition of other areas, including parts of Central America, South America and Southeast Asia, it seems likely that the total rural population living in tropical environments of marked climatic seasonality will be over one billion. This represents a high proportion of the very poor people in the world.

Malnutrition, morbidity and mortality have seasonal patterns and often peak during the wet season   Patterns of seasonal stress vary. In pastoral areas of very low rainfall, the most critical times of the year are usually towards the end of the dry season (see for example, Swift, 1981[3]). In North India the very hot dry season, the hot wet season, and the cold dry season are all associated with different forms of stress and morbidity. Elsewhere in the tropics the most difficult time of year appears very generally to be the wet season. This is sometimes reflected in local terms: Papua New Guineans often refer to the wet and dry seasons as 'taem nogut' and 'gutpela taem' respectively (R.M. Bourke, personal communication). For cultivators and labourers the rains are often a 'lean' or 'hungry' period of physical stress when shortages of food combine with high energy demand for agricultural activities (Bayliss-Smith, 1981, Longhurst and Payne, 1979). Food is at its scarcest, most expensive, least varied, and least well prepared at these times of year (Schofield, 1974). Resistance to disease is lowered.

But it is precisely at this time that exposure to infection is often most pronounced and morbidity highest. While there are local variations and exceptions, it is common during tropical rains for there to be a rise in the incidence of diarrhoeas (Chowdhury *et al.*, 1981; Cutting, 1981, Drasar *et al.*, 1981; Rowland *et al.*, 1981), malaria (Bray, 1981), skin infections (Porter, 1981), guinea worm disease (Belcher *et al.*, 1975; Muller, 1981), dengue fever (Halstead, 1966), and snake bites (Warrell and Arnett, 1976).[4] Other diseases may also be most prevalent at these times, as with cholera in parts of Bangladesh (Chowdhury *et al.*, 1981). Not only is morbidity high at these times, but death rates in tropical countries typically peak during or just after the rains (Dyson and Crook, 1981). The wet season is not just the hungry season; it is also often the sick season.

The poorer people, women and children are especially vulnerable to hardship, malnutrition, sickness and death in the wet season   Seasonal malnutrition and poverty go together and for many of the poorer people, seasonal shortages of food coincide with a demand for high energy output in agricultural activities. This is reflected in substantial changes in body weight in areas of seasonality and poverty (Hunter, 1967; Longhurst and Payne, 1979). Body-weight data have, however, rarely been analysed by socio-economic category. In the one case that is known, Chowdhury and others (1981) found in one part of Bangladesh that landless mothers had lower average body weights, and greater variance seasonally around the mean, than did mothers in families with two acres of land or more.[5] On the

42

basis of extensive comparative analysis, Schofield has written (1974:25) that '. . . the very poor do more physical work and get less food, and the short- and long-term effects of seasonal variations around an already low level are thus worse for poor families.'

Mortality is also, as might be expected, higher among poorer people. This is notoriously so during famine, and is illustrated by McCord's much quoted evidence from Companiganj in Bangladesh in 1975 in the sequel to the floods of 1974. He found that the crude death rate was three times higher among landless families than among those with three or more acres of land, while the differential increased to five times for deaths of children aged 1–4 years – 86.5 per 1,000 among landless families, compared with 17.5 per 1,000 among families with three acres or more (McCord, 1976, cited in Chowdhury and Chen, 1977:417). Perhaps more remarkable is the finding of Durham (pers. comm.) that in a rural area in El Salvador the child mortality rate of children of females born between 1915 and 1945 was about 38 per cent among landless families compared with about 11 per cent for families with two hectares or more. As we have noted (Dyson and Crook, 1981), mortality is also seasonal. The question then arises whether seasonal peaks in mortality disproportionately represent poorer people, women, and/or children.

The evidence available is suggestive. McGregor and others, for example, found that half the infant deaths in a Gambian village occurred during the three months of the rains (McGregor et al., 1961, and McGregor, 1976). A report of the work of the Dunn Nutritional Unit, Cambridge's work in the Gambia states that 'A positive correlation was found between infant mor- tality and good rainfall and between infant mortality and a good harvest. Infant mortality was higher because in a good harvest the women had less time to care for the children who developed diarrhoea and more measles' (IDRC, 1980:22). It seems reasonable to suppose that maternal neglect and infant deaths in such situations will be greatest among those for whom it is most imperative to work, and they are likely to be the poorest. Similarly, Becker and Sardar, analysing data from Matlab Thana in Bangladesh, found that the age groups with the most marked seasonality of death were those in which the overall risk of death was high. They reported that these were children in the first month and first year of life, and people aged 44 and above. Within these age groups families which are landless seem to be the most vulnerable to sharp fluctuations in deaths, perhaps reflecting their very precarious financial position in slack months prior to harvest (Becker and Sardar, 1981). Given the interactions between poverty, malnutrition, mor- bidity and seasonality, it would indeed be surprising if this were not the case.

Part of the difficulty in writing about seasonal privation is the multiple linkages which operate at the worst times. This can be illustrated by some aspects which especially concern women and children (see Schofield, 1974, PAG of the UN 1977, Chowdhury et al., 1981, Palmer, 1981, Rowland et al., 1981, Whitehead et al., 1978, Schofield, 1979). It is possible that some lactating women stop breastfeeding with the onset of the rains, anticipating hard work, but increasing the risks for their weaned children at the time of peak exposure (see for example, Barrell and Rowland, 1979) to bacterial

43

overgrowth of foods. Within the family, women may also be discriminated against in the allocations of food. In the Gambia, Whitehead and others found (1978:5–7) a sharply reduced capacity for lactation during the rains when mothers' average intakes fell to less than 50 per cent of the recommended value. In the month of August they found that women in the last trimester of pregnancy lost an average of 1.4 kg, and that a similar weight loss occurred during lactation at that time. During the rains, women often have exceptionally heavy work loads, which leads to stress and to the neglect of children and of domestic activities generally. Schofield has listed some effects of re-allocating female labour time during this period of crisis:

> *Cooking practices* change, especially where quick easy-to-prepare meals (usually of the nutritionally poorer staples such as cassava) are produced once a day or in bulk, and vitamins are destroyed by food kept simmering in the pot. *Intra-family distribution of food* is affected, where the children are asleep before the daily meal has been prepared and women have no time to either prepare special infant foods or effect the proper distribution of available foods. *Food gathering* may be inhibited so that some types of foods (e.g. green leafy vegetables) are suddenly excluded from the diet. *House-cleaning*, essential in overcrowded and insanitary conditions, may be inhibited. *Fuel and water* collection is constrained by lack of time. Finally mothers devote less time to the *care* of their children who are often left in charge of other siblings or elderly grandparents.
>
> (Schofield, 1974:27, *emphases in original*)

A further condition which appears adverse for mothers and children is the tendency for births to peak in the late rains and around the time of harvest. There is evidence for this from widely scattered environments including Bangladesh (Becker and Sardar, 1981), Guatemala (Mata, 1978:34), most states in India (Dyson and Crook, 1981), Nigeria (pers. comm., Richard Longhurst), and Senegal (Lericollais, 1972:14). The questions here are complex, and birth at any time of the year has its particular disadvantages. A careful analysis by Schofield (1979:102–9) finds no simple conclusion about a best time for births. Each environment is likely to deserve separate examination. But a concurrence of late pregnancy with heavy work, food shortages, poor nutrition, and high exposure to infections during the rains and around harvest, is hard for both mothers and babies. Rowland and others (1981) found in the Gambia that birth weights during the six months which included the rains were significantly lower than for the other six months of the year. The prognosis for those children born during the rains was also worse. Rowland and his collaborators have written, in summary, that 'many adverse factors operate mainly during one period of the year, the rainy season. The mother who produces her child at this time will have suffered more weight loss herself during pregnancy, producing a smaller child who then gets less breast milk and cannot "catch up" ' (1978:9). To the extent that late pregnancy and birth peak at a time of year which is difficult for the mother and which offers a poor prognosis for the child, this is yet another way in which tropical seasonality accentuates the stress and risks of the vulnerable.

The economic costs of sickness and weakness are concentrated in the wet season The economic costs of sickness and weakness can be analysed both in terms of agricultural production foregone in the economy, and in terms of losses for small-farming and landless families.

These costs are linked with the seasonal labour demands of tropical agriculture. These are often sharply peaked, especially for the activities of land preparation, transplanting, weeding and harvesting. For small-farming families, the area they can cultivate and the yield they can obtain depend on adequate and timely labour inputs. As Hugh Bunting has written,

> In many traditional farming systems, particularly in the seasonally arid tropics, there are pronounced seasonal peaks in the demand for labour, notably in the early part of the season when land must be broken and crops sown and weeded. The peak is accentuated by the risks of losing the initial flush of nitrogen to leaching on the one hand and to weeds on the other. (1970:737)

Inability to carry out an operation promptly can, then, mean loss of a crop. In the words of a Gambia village woman to Margaret Haswell, 'sometimes you are overcome by weeds through illness or accidents' (Haswell, 1975:44). With small farmers who have to rely on family labour, and for whom that labour limits area or yield, incapacity through illness is likely to mean a smaller crop or no crop at all.

Such incapacity is most obvious in those diseases which are epidemic during and just after the rains, as with malaria and guinea worm disease. The effects of malaria have long been recognised. Thus B.H. Farmer, in his classic study of the Dry Zone of Ceylon, wrote:

> In addition to its effect on the death-rate and on the ability of the Dry Zone population to maintain itself, malaria induced mental and physical inefficiency in its victims. The incidence of fever was unfortunately highest during the rainy season . . . just when the stricken cultivators should have been busy with their . . . main paddy crop and with their *chenas* (dryland cultivation). It is not surprising that general debility and seasonal fever helped, with other factors, to produce low crop yields. (Farmer, 1957:20)

The major reduction in malaria in the Dry Zone was, he considered, 'a true revolution' (ibid.:223).

Guinea worm disease presents another dramatic example of loss of production through incapacity. Belcher and others (1975) considered, on the basis of a study in rural Ghana, that this was the major preventable cause of agricultural work loss. They reported that

> The highest attack rate was in adult male farmers, with three out of four affected in some villages. Disease which occurs at a slack period would have little impact on agricultural output, but guinea worm disease coincides with the two peak agricultural periods. Untreated farmers were completely disabled for over five weeks, and few households succeeded

in finding alternative labour sources so that a major crop was lost. (Belcher *et al.*, 1975:248)

They concluded that 'Because guinea worm disease is seasonal, coinciding with peak agricultural activities, and few alternative labour sources are available for the incapacitated farmer, a marked reduction in agricultural output occurs' (ibid.:243).

The diarrhoeas may be somewhat more varied in their seasonalities than either malaria or guinea worm disease, and their effects are less visible. But they are so widespread, with an estimated three to five billion infections per annum in the world (Walsh and Warren, 1979: appendix A), that it is difficult to imagine that they do not contribute substantially to losses in production. Infections of the skin also tend to be less spectacular, but bacterial and fungal infections are most prevalent during the rains and skin diseases are a frequent reason for people visiting health facilities. They affect how time is utilized in the family and they too have direct and indirect economic costs (Porter, 1981). Indeed, production is liable to be affected not just by those diseases which have pronounced peaks during the agricultural season, but by all diseases, whether they peak or not, which weaken or incapacitate at this time.

Moreover, it may often be the interaction of several adverse factors, of which a specific disease is but one, which reduce work. Margaret Haswell has observed of a village in the Gambia: 'persistently poor feeding and lowered resistance to disease adversely affected the quality of work of some farmers' (1975:45). The cost in production and income foregone is often the outcome of interactions of malnutrition, high-energy demand, low immune response, and combinations and sequences of morbidity.

If the economic costs of incapacity to work, and therefore the benefits of prevention of incapacity, are highly seasonal, the estimation of these costs and benefits is far from simple, and subject to many local variations and subtleties. Nicholas Prescott, after reviewing ten attempts to evaluate the social costs of malaria and the social benefits of its control in particular communities, concludes that 'no cost-benefit analysis of malaria control has yet provided a plausible estimate of the net aggregate income benefit which might result' (1979:39). Prescott argues that the benefits of malaria control may have been exaggerated through high values for the duration of disability and debility per case, and through ignoring the seasonal distribution of cases in relation to seasonal labour surpluses (1979:66). Responses to malaria at peak periods include: working in spite of it (though with diminished efficiency); pressing into service other family members; and employing non-family labour. He also argues that 'cases prevented in periods of labour surplus will probably contribute a zero marginal product' (1979:66), repeating a point made earlier by Elliott that if acute sickness strikes during a period of excess family labour capacity, its economic cost is zero (1970:655).

The reality may often be more complex. First, any analysis of social costs and benefits of labour inputs foregone must be in terms of farming calendars and the benefits of timeliness. A farming family suffering sickness during a critical week, even if other labour is eventually recruited or pressed into service, may suffer a major loss of production which is easily underestimated. Second, sickness in a slack period may not be costless: it may have a lingering or permanent effect on physical capacity, or it may require payments for treatment which impoverish and which reduce the ability to cope with subsequent seasonal peaks. For both these reasons, the benefits of incapacity averted will be higher rather than lower.

For families, the costs and benefits to small farmers may sometimes differ from those to landless labourers. Higher wages at times of peak labour demand, especially harvest, suggest high costs to labourers from being sick at those times. This may be generally true, and supports the case for seasonal preventive interventions. However, two possible twists may be noted. The first is that less sickness among small farmers at times of peak labour demand may reduce employment for the landless, since farm families will be better able to meet their requirements from their own resources: for example, Bhambore and others (1952, cited in Prescott, 1979:24) found in one village in a malarious area in Mysore that after an anti-malarial programme, annual expenditure on hired labour fell by 76 per cent in one sprayed village for which data were available. The second possible twist is that for very poor people in zones of marked labour surplus – as in parts of Indonesia (Benjamin White, personal communication) – it may take more hours of work in the slack season to earn enough to survive than it takes in the busy season. For a very poor family with one or more members sick, it may then be harder to obtain enough for survival in the slack season that it is in the busy season, so that slack season sickness brings greater privation. While these two twists may be exceptional, the possibility of their occurrence deserves to be on the agenda of rural planning where there are landless labourers.

In general, however, the evidence is strong that the costs of sickness and weakness for rural agricultural populations are usually concentrated in the wet season. The implications for rural health planning are both immediate and future. One objective of rural planning in areas of labour surplus is to create labour scarcities which will drive up real wages and differentially benefit the landless and near-landless. As scarcities are created, the costs in production foregone of sickness at peak periods will rise sharply. One example is the watershed technology being developed by the International Crops Research Institute for the Semi-Arid Tropics (ICRISAT) at Hyderabad. Although there are seasonal health problems in ICRISAT survey villages, they have not been presented as a major problem limiting agricultural production. But the new watershed technology would shift labour demand from a position where on average all demands can be met from family labour throughout the year, to one in which there would be acutely peaked deficits (Ghodake et al., 1978). One may speculate whether with such a technology villagers might not come to perceive illness at those times as a new serious problem; certainly the economic returns to effective preventive health programmes at those times would rise with the change in farming system. In such a case, as generally, costs to society and to families of incapacity through sickness will be higher wherever there is a labour deficit at times of seasonal demand, so often precisely when vulnerability to sickness is greatest.

It is during the wet season that sickness is most liable to make people permanently poorer Rural poverty has many causes, and discussion of seasonality should not distract attention from those which are political and social, or from political and social solutions. At the same time, in seeking to slow, arrest or reverse processes of impoverishment, it is relevant to analyse the contingencies which trigger loss of assets or the incurring of debts. These are very obvious to the people concerned, but few recent studies are known which have analysed the proximate events which provoke the sale or mortgaging of land, livestock, jewellery, utensils, or tools, or the negotiation of loans. These contingencies can be classified as social and ceremonial (bride-wealth, dowry, weddings, funerals etc); legal (litigation, compensation and fines); consumption (alcoholism, etc); failures of enterprises; famine; and sickness.

A distinction can be made here between ways in which tropical seasons help to keep people poor, screwing them down cyclically in their poverty; and ways in which tropical seasons may make people poorer, forcing them down past a ratchet which may be irreversible. Mild or brief sickness may merely reinforce the cyclical screw, though the poorer people are, the more serious it is likely to be; but acute or prolonged sickness is more likely to force a ratchet, to be a contingency which impoverishes permanently.

The relative significance of health ratchet effects in processes of impoverishment can be expected to vary according to the levels of other contingencies, the degrees of poverty, the incidence and seriousness of disease, the availability and efficacy of curative facilities, and the direct and indirect costs of treatment. The severe and irreversible effects of even quite a short illness can be illustrated by the example of a landless family in the Philippines, the Sumagaysays. Tiyo Oyo, the head of the family, was stricken by a mild form of cholera for a month, and had to be taken to hospital. Tiya Teria, his wife, handled the crisis. Antonio Ledesma reports:

> The week's stay in hospital cost the family P120, with food not yet included. Another P130 had to be provided to buy dextrose when Tiyo Oyo was in a critical condition. Fortunately, one of the drugstores in Pototan agreed to provide a guarantee for the Sumagaysays in the hospital. To cover the expenses, Tiya Teria had to sell their carabao (buffalo) for P330 to another small farmer . . . The carabao was already in full working condition, and under normal circumstances could have been sold for more than twice the amount received by the Sumagaysays. Moreover, with the carabao, Tiyo Oyo would still have been able to plough other farm parcels for P10 a day instead of working as a pure manual labourer for the current wage rate of P6 a day . . . In that sense, parting with the carabao meant parting with their last capital investment in farming. Buying a new carabao today would be unthinkable with the current market value of a working carabao estimated at P1,000–1,500. (Ledesma, 1977:27)

One may note, in this example, what may be common: the high cost of treatment, the need for cash at short notice to meet it, the distress sale of an asset at less than its normal market value, the reduced family earning capacity as a result of the sale, and the impossibility of ever regaining the asset. A short illness can make a family permanently poorer, as it did with the Sumagaysays.

The incidence of such health ratchet effects is difficult to assess. An illustration can be drawn from a micro-study by David Parkin in a coastal area of Kenya. He has written:

Natural or man-made misfortunes, of which the greatest is sickness, strike into the lives or men and their families with a suddenness which defies resistance or delay. Cures must be sought, sometimes at great expense, from a range of traditional doctors, whose various techniques are applied until success, or death, ensues. (Parkin, 1972:59–60)

Parkin found that sickness was a common reason for selling land, being given or implied as a factor in 14 out of 58 transactions (pp.60–61). He concluded that 'Bride-wealth demands, sickness, and death . . . are the main factors prompting men to dispose permanently of their palms and land' (ibid.:61). Similarly, in Bangladesh, sickness appears to be a common factor leading to the impoverishment of families, and especially of women whose husbands have died after an illness during which the family's assets have been sold seeking treatment and cure.[6] One may speculate about how many millions of families, each year, are made permanently poorer by the costs of sickness and treatment; how preventable this may be; and how, through these processes, 'sickness begets sickness' (Elliott, 1980:73).

These examples do not indicate the seasons when the sicknesses occurred. They might have been at any time of the year. But there are reasons for supposing that ratchet effects from sickness are most common and are most commonly precipitated, during the lean and vulnerable season of the rains. It is not just that the incidence of disease is often greater then. Perhaps more, it is that other factors interact to make sickness more damaging at that time. During the agricultural slack season, after harvest, families have more resources to meet the costs of treatment and transport, travel is relatively easy, the labour of the sick person and of those who take the person for treatment has low opportunity cost, the climate is usually more favourable for recovery, food is adequate and more varied, and time can be spared to care for the sick person. In contrast, during the busy and lean agricultural season, families have fewer resources to meet costs of treatment and transport, travel is more difficult, the labour of the sick person and of those who take the person for treatment has high opportunity cost, the climate is less favourable for recovery, food is often scarce and less varied, and time is harder to spare to care for the sick person. In the lean season of the rains, then, it is likely that there will be longer delays before treatment (if any), that sickness will last longer, and that the costs, direct and indirect, will be much higher. Sickness during the rains and before harvest is thus more likely to lead to irreversible impoverishment. Not only is the incidence of sickness higher; it is also more damaging. More than at other times sickness in the wet season is liable to make poor people permanently poorer.

Rural health services are likely to be at their least effective in the wet season In order to prevent and treat sickness, to reduce mortality, to help the poorer people, women and children, to reduce the economic costs of sickness, and to prevent people being made permanently poorer by sickness, rural health services should be at their most effective during the time of greatest need, typically in the wet season. This is, however, when they are likely to be least effective. There is an agenda of possible factors to be addressed in any particular situation:

(a) the demand for medicaments may be high, but supplies are often on a flat rate monthly basis. At these times, then, if there is any shortage, more people will go without treatment. (If there is an unofficial inducement paid for treatment, this may seasonally rise to reflect the excess of demand over supply, discriminating against those who find it hard to pay);

(b) the supply of medicaments may be interrupted by problems of transport during the rains. Supplies to meet emergencies will be harder to get through than at other times of the year;

(c) standards may fall because supervisors visit less because of transport problems;

(d) there will be less specialist treatment of serious cases either on the spot or through referral because of transport and other communication problems;

(e) mobile services may not be able to operate, or be able to operate only on good roads;

(f) health staff may take leave, or devote less of their time to health work, in order to fulfil the competing demands of their own agricultural activities. This may apply especially with village primary health-care workers;

(g) health staff (especially primary health-care workers who may be subject to many of the seasonal stresses) may themselves be sick at these times of year;

(h) inelastic services will deal with a lower proportion of those in need at times of high demand that in slack periods;

(i) (as we have seen) rural people may be less able to reach or afford to take up health services during the rains;

(j) there may be a problem with the phasing of the financial year. Funds are typically short in the second half of any financial year, and especially so towards the end of it. In countries in East Africa, for example, where the long rains begin in March or April, a financial year which starts in July may mean that drugs and transport are in short supply at precisely the time when they are most needed.

Urban-based professionals underperceive seasonal deprivation and underestimate morbidity in the wet season To the extent that the six preceding propositions apply, one would expect rural health services, both preventive and curative, to anticipate the demands of coming wet seasons and to pay special attention to those diseases most prevalent and incapacitating at those times and to those who are most vulnerable. Informal evidence suggests that this is rare. It seems odd, given the strong influence of economists on planning, that health services should not be concentrated on the period when they are most cost-effective in preventing the loss of agricultural production. In its section on health as a productive investment, the World Bank's Health Sector Policy paper shows no awareness of this but is, rather preoccupied with the costs of 'absenteeism' (World Bank, 1975:25–9), suggesting an urban, plantation and large-farm bias. It also seems odd, given the fieldwork of sociologists and social anthropologists which extends through several seasons, that more attention should not have been directed towards the need for health services at those times when sickness is most likely to impoverish. There is something to explain. Either the propositions are false or exaggerated, or there must be reasons why their implications are not perceived or pursued. If such reasons exist, the propositions are all the more credible.

Four biases[7] do indeed appear to operate so that professionals underperceive seasonal deprivation and underestimate morbidity during the wet season:

Professional and personal biases
Medical practitioners are pointed away from rural poverty and seasonality by their professional training and by their life experiences. Professional training has been influenced by needs in highly industrialized rich countries in temperate climates, where urban living provides little contact with rural seasonality, food shortages are rare, and harvest, the main agricultural labour peak, comes at a healthy time of year. Professional training for specialized expertise tends to concentrate and narrow vision, so that if professionals (whether medical or other) do note adverse seasonal effects, these tend to be limited to their restricted preoccupations. A doctor may observe seasonal patterns of morbidity but not of indebtedness. An economist may analyse seasonal changes in wages but not in the incidence of malaria. For rural people, unblinkered by disciplinary specialization, multiple adverse seasonal interactions may be more obvious. But professionals have been trained away from being able to see them, and have been so 'educated' that they are often neither able nor willing to learn from rural people.[8] Professional insight into the multiple interactions of adverse seasonality is one of the casualties. This is reinforced by the well-known urban bias of professionals generally and of doctors in particular. For many, urban work is most professionally satisfying, most remunerative, and most convenient. Professionally and personally, and except for a small but distinguished minority, doctors are not exposed to rural seasonality and so do not appreciate its significance.

Biases of access and contact
Areas visited by urban-based professionals tend to be those that are more accessible – urban, peri-urban, and regions near large cities (which tend to

51

be the more prosperous). This has been described as 'tarmac bias'. Ssenny-onga has observed in Kenya how services are concentrated along good roads, how the better-off people buy up plots there and build good houses, and how the poorer people move back out of sight (Ssennyonga, 1976:9–10, and personal communication). Those contacted on rural visits by urban-based professionals are likely to be those who are less adversely affected by seasonality – those who are accessible and visible, the better-off rather than the poorer, people on regular salaries rather than people depending on agriculture, farmers rather than labourers, people with access to off-farm employment rather than those dependent solely on cultivation, men more than women, those in project areas rather than those outside, users of services rather than non-users, those who go to meetings rather than those who stay at home, those who go to market (who have something to sell, or something with which to buy) rather than those who do not go because they have nothing, those who are alive not those who have died. Those most affected by adverse seasonality are precisely those least likely to be encountered.

Dry season bias
Rural visits by urban-based professionals have their own seasonality. Epidemiologists *may* visit during the rains. But for urban people generally, the rains are a bad time for rural travel because of floods, mud, broken bridges, getting stuck, damaging vehicles, losing time, and enduring discomfort. In some places, roads are officially closed. In South Sudan, there is a period of about two months after the onset of the rains when roads are impassable but when there is not yet enough water in the rivers for travel by boat. Many rural areas are quite simply inaccessible by vehicle during the rains. The worst times of year are then not seen. But once the rains are over, urban-based professionals travel more freely. The dry season, when disease is diminishing, food stocks are adequate, body weights are rising, cere-monies are in full swing, and people are at their least deprived, is the peak period for rural visits, forming impressions, and gathering data.[9] Even nutrition surveys are sometimes carried out after the harvest (Jim Pines, personal communication).

Statistical biases
Two sets of statistical biases understate the incidence of sickness during rains. First, even where surveys are carried out all round the year, analysis of the data tends to be aggregate. Only if time, patience, money and inter-est are adequate (which they often are not), will the more time-consuming analysis which shows seasonal variations be carried out.

Second, and more seriously, there are many reasons why sickness in the wet season is under-reported in official statistics. An example of under-reporting of a seasonally crippling disease is presented by Belcher and others. In their study of guinea worm disease in Ghana they observed that attendance at modern health facilities was low because of distances in-volved, increased pain with motion, and greater reliance upon traditional medicines (1975:248). They found that 'few infected persons attend medical clinics (less than one per cent in this study) so that its incidence is greatly underestimated' (p.243). The question here, as more generally, is why there is under-reporting and what seasonal factors affect it. Many factors alone or combined, can be expected to reduce the proportion of the sick who get to health posts or clinics or hospitals during the rains, and who therefore appear in the statistics: difficulties and discomforts of travel (impassable roads, mud, floods, rains, etc.); shortages of cash; the high cost of loans during the lean season; the high cost of time and energy required to get sick people to treatment during food shortages and agricultural activities;[10] the high cost of waiting for treatment;[11] longer waiting times for treatment; inelastic services;[12] multiple under-nutrition and sickness in the same family; delays in treatment leading to greater incapacity, greater pain, and greater difficulty in movement; and sheer physical weakness and exhaustion in both the sick and their helpers. These factors interact, and the distortion is accentuated by the operation of their opposites during a dry season following harvest.[13] Not only do these statistical warps understate wet season sickness but they reinforce other biases, making it even more difficult for professionals who are trained to use statistics to appreciate the extent and seriousness of seasonal morbidity.[14]

When these biases – personal and professional, access and contact, dry season, and statistical – are seen to be interacting with and reinforcing one another, it is less difficult to understand why seasonal dimensions of health and poverty are not more prominent in health programmes.

Practical implications

This analysis has its own biases. It has been influenced especially by three sets and sequences of studies in three rural environments of marked seasonality in respectively, the Gambia,[15] Northern Nigeria,[16] and Bangladesh.[17] Other environments are less seasonal, or more seasonal, or seasonal in different combinations of ways. In particular, the cold dry – hot dry – hot wet seasonality of much of Northern India presents a pattern of stress in the hot dry season which qualifies the scenario. It cannot be emphasised too strongly that each rural situation should be appraised separately to identify what interventions are appropriate. The practical implications which follow are not a blueprint. They are, rather, a checklist of ideas and a repertoire of options to consider, environment by environment.

Practical implications can be suggested under the headings of research, health services, and rural planning and action.

Research
Enough is known already, or enough is easily knowable through local-level analysis, for many seasonal problems to be tackled. Moreover, research can be a distraction, an excuse for postponement, and a means of reinforcing vertical and technological approaches to health problems which may distract from the priority of horizontal emphasis on primary health care. All the same, much remains to be known and done. Four suggestions can be made for research.

Sickness and impoverishment   This research could be cheap, simple and widespread. It would rely heavily on the knowledge of rural people. The objective would be to identify the relative importance of seasonal sickness among other proximate factors in processes of impoverishment. It would involve both counting, as carried out by Parkin (1972) in Kenya, and case studies, like that written up by Ledesma (1977) from the Philippines. Besides its value as a contribution to knowledge, this approach should also be a useful part of local-level seasonal analysis in rural planning.

Micro-level seasonal linkages   This would be more complex, involving analysis across disciplines to identify seasonal interactions, especially between bio-medical, socio-economic, and agricultural factors. It would rely on adding socio-economic and agricultural dimensions to existing bio-medical research (for example, in the Gambia and Bangladesh), or in adding bio-medical dimensions to existing socio-economic and agricultural research (as with the villages studies by ICRISAT). Since there is already a strong data base in these studies, the marginal additions to knowledge might be high indeed, illuminating relationships between morbidity, mortality, age groups, socio-economic categories, seasons, and agriculture, and leading towards insights which might permit simpler diagnosis and prevention for rural planning and action elsewhere.

Seasonal mapping   At an early stage in planning counter-seasonal strategies, it would be useful to map the spatial distribution of adverse seasonal factors and their linkages. In Sri Lanka, for example, the seasonality of malaria differs between ecological zones. Elsewhere, there may be acute combinations of adverse factors which are simultaneous in their impact only in certain definable regions. A preliminary mapping of seasonal interactions within a region or country should indicate those zones where attention should initially be directed.

Research on tropical diseases   Whatever the reservations that a vertical approach may divert attention from primary health care, the global figure of about US$60 million (Walsh and Warren, 1979:20) for research on tropical diseases looks low. The UNDP/World Bank/WHO Special Programme for Research and Training in Tropical Diseases (covering malaria, schistosomiasis, filariasis, trypanosomiasis, leishmaniasis, and leprosy) and the International Centre for Diarrheal Disease Research in Bangladesh are, though belated, major new thrusts. The priorities accorded to malaria and the diarrhoeas fit the seasonal priorities which follow from the arguments in this chapter. The question remains, however, to what extent the needs and wishes of rural people weigh as against professional considerations in determining research priorities, and whether the high costs, both social and private, of incapacity at periods of agricultural activity are taken into account. The rarity with which a seasonal link between health and agriculture is noted in medical writing about rural health suggests that the weight is less than it should be. In selecting future priorities, seasonal analysis argues for priority for those diseases

54

and complaints which weaken and incapacitate most at times of food shortage and high labour demand.

Health services
Seasonal analysis of health, agriculture and poverty has implications for the planning and operation of rural health services, and especially for the priority (WHO 1978) of effective primary health care. The seasonal dimension is, of course, only one of several. It may be argued that there are sometimes, or often, other priorities; that if, as found in a part of rural Ghana (IDS Health Group 1978), a third to a half of the population of districts live out of effective reach of health units providing primary care, it may be more important first to extend coverage before refining it to take account of seasonality. On the other hand, if a programme meets felt needs, as seasonal preventive and curative measures may often do, it will be popular, there will be a demand for it, staff morale and better staff performance may result, and there may be many benefits, notably for the poor.

Some of the more obvious suggestions arising from the analysis in this chapter are:

- stocking rural clinics and health posts with medicaments on a seasonal basis to meet seasonal needs, especially in preparation for the rains. This is a particular priority for primary health care in areas which are cut off in the wet season.
- priority for seasonal preventive measures against diseases which incapacitate during the wet season. Malaria is a notable case where much can be achieved for relatively low cost and with enthusiastic public support. An example is seasonal anti-malarial chemoprophylaxis combined with other preventive measures in Raigarh District, Madhya Pradesh, where in two years an incidence believed to have been about 95 per cent was brought down to almost nil, with poor people prepared to pay for their pills (Sister Lorraine Ryan, personal communication). The cost-effectiveness of chemoprophylactic anti-malarial programmes can also be increased by shifting from year-round to seasonal implementation, as in some parts of Mozambique where action is being concentrated on the seasons of highest incidence (Malcolm Segall, personal communication).
- priority for seasonal curative facilities for those sicknesses, especially diarrhoeas, malaria, skin infections, guinea worm disease, and dengue fever, which tend to be most prevalent during the wet season.
- caution in introducing mobile clinics. Mobile clinics have been questioned on other grounds. The additional seasonal argument is that they may be unable to reach the more remote people who are often poorer and more vulnerable to adverse seasonality;[18] and that during the rains, when health services are most needed in less accessible places, mobile clinics will be at their least mobile, often confined to tarmac roads, if not to garages.
- concentrating preventive and curative health services in areas where the costs (in production foregone, in suffering, in impoverishment) of sickness in the sick and hungry season are highest.

55

- encouragement of child day-care facilities especially at times of stress when mothers have to work in the fields. This has been done successfully in several, perhaps many, places. For example, harvest-season day-care centres were an effective addition to the Narangwal Project child health programme in the Indian Punjab (Robert L. Parker, personal communication).
- in family welfare programmes, discussing the best and worst times of the year to give birth. Rural women may often be much more aware of the advantages or disadvantages of different seasons for birth than urban-based professionals realize. Discussing desirable times may provide one focus among others for enabling rural women to see advantages in being able to control fertility.
- concentrating health education and preventive programmes such as immunization in the dry season. This is when rural people usually have more time, when their time has a low opportunity cost, and when they are in better health and have higher immune response. Health staff may also have a lower work-load at that time, and travelling conditions are better.
- staffing on a seasonal basis (in timing leave, in shifting staff from one area to another) in order to meet local seasonal needs. This may, however, be a difficult refinement to implement. It has been tried in Matlab Thana in Bangladesh, where Chowdhury and others (1981) report:

  Seasonal diarrhoea in Matlab has prompted the ICDDR (International Centre for Diarrheal Disease Research) hospital to shift staff between periods of strong and weak service demand. Preventive work and non-seasonal curative services, such as family planning, may be undertaken during non-epidemic periods. It should be stressed, however, that this increase of staff efficiency may be achieved only at the cost of increased programme complexity. Shifting of staff required more training, supervision, and other programme support services.

- Selecting community health workers for primary health care who are less, rather than more, dependent on agricultural activities, so that they will be less distracted from health work at the times of greatest need. Seasonal analysis leans here against that conventional wisdom which holds that community health workers should be part-time farmers, typical members of the community, and unpaid. If a community faces a seasonal crisis simultaneously in cultivation and in health, a community health worker in a farming family may be torn between conflicting obligations, and those of cultivation for the family may prevail over those of health for the community. In planning primary health care, and in selecting community health workers, this is a factor to be borne in mind.

Rural planning and action
As noted above, the perceptions of urban-based professionals are distorted by biases (personal, professional, access, contact, dry season, and statistical) so that they either fail to recognize or underestimate seasonal linkages and seasonal deprivation. Rural planning, notably in health, has anyway a

56

tendency to emphasize location and buildings rather than implementation and timing. But past neglect is present opportunity. Precisely because seasonality has been missed as a link between health, agriculture and poverty, it now presents potential for seasonal programmes to counter poverty and deprivation.

Such programmes have to be tailored to particular rural environments. This implies decentralization. One approach is a required procedure for local-level staff to carry out seasonal analysis.[19] Health and agricultural staff might be required jointly with each other and with rural people to identify seasonal linkages between health, nutrition, agriculture and poverty in the areas in which they work. Particular attention might be paid to the views and experience of those poorer rural people most adversely affected. The incentives to staff might be enhanced by workshops with their colleagues from other areas to which their findings were reported, and then by together working out and agreeing proposals for action. Such joint analysis and action can be suggested for the district and sub-district level. This procedure should heighten awareness of seasonal problems, leading to health programmes and other interventions better geared to the seasonal needs of agriculture and of the poorer people.

Implementation is the crux. Good ideas which are not implementable are bad ideas. The best way forward may be to develop methods of seasonal analysis and a repertoire of interventions which are simple, manageable, replicable and effective, and which involve rural people as partners. Analysis is the easier part; the greater challenge is action. Ways forward may be sought through combinations of decentralized seasonal analysis, action programmes, evaluation, and then training and replication. In such ways, if this chapter is correct, much might be done to restrain processes of impoverishment, to increase agricultural production, and to benefit those who are poorer and weaker. This could be achieved, moreover, without significant loss, and often with gains, to those rural people who are less poor and more powerful. The local political obstacles which so often impede and subvert programmes intended to benefit the rural poor should therefore be less serious than usual, and may not appear at all. Seasonal analysis and action should, then, benefit those most in need, making things better for them at the times they find worst.

Postscript

Since this chapter was published as an article in 1982, more light has been thrown on tropical seasonality and its adverse effects. Much of the new evidence has reinforced the seven propositions in the article.

Some of the main developments and new sources are the following. Also in 1982, an Eastern African workshop brought together contributions published as *A Report on the Regional Workshop on Seasonal Variations in the Provisioning, Nutrition and Health of Rural Families* (Jiggins, 1982). In the same year, Roe and Fortmann produced their monograph *Season and Strategy: the changing organization of the rural water sector in Botswana* which explored seasonality in the functioning of organizations and in resource management, and showed how official perceptions of overstocking could be distorted by a failure to appreciate the seasonality of water availability and use. In 1985, a workshop convened by the Institute of Development Studies, Sussex led to *Seasonality and Poverty* (Longhurst, 1986), an IDS Bulletin which included papers on ultrapoverty (Lipton), women (Jiggins), pastoralism (White), household food strategies (Longhurst, Toulmin), biomass and plants (Leakey), trees (Chambers and Longhurst) and primary health care (Gordon). This was followed by a conference convened by IFPRI which led to a volume entitled *Seasonal Variability in Third World Agriculture: The Consequences for Food Security* (Sahn, 1989). This explores the seasonality of household food security, examining the extent, patterns, causes and consequences of seasonal variations in wages, agricultural earnings, food availability, prices, consumption, and nutritional status; the stability and predictability of seasonal cycles; and links with grain marketing, technology and policy. Two other publications have examined how rural people manage seasonal stress: *Coping with Seasonal Constraints* (Huss-Ashmore et al., 1988) consists of ten papers, including analysis from fieldwork in Peru, Lesotho, Botswana, Sierra Leone, Burkina Faso and Niger; and Martha Alter Chen's book *Coping with Seasonality and Drought* (Chen, 1991) reports on field research in Gujarat. Most comprehensively, Gerard Gill's book *Seasonality and Agriculture in the Developing World: A problem of the poor and powerless* (Gill, 1991a) has brought together a mass of evidence covering a wide range of topics, among them some which had been relatively neglected such as intra-household disparities, labour migration, credit, and prices. Gill's book also includes a useful 15 pages of references and sources.

Two qualifications to the seven propositions have been presented and are of interest.

First, Walker and Ryan's *Village and Household Economies in India's Semi-arid Tropics* (Walker and Ryan, 1990) analyses longitudinal data from six villages and brings to light local variations in seasonal characteristics, showing for example related variations in soil type, timing of agricultural operations, labour demand, and food availability. They also found rather little seasonal variation in nutritional status. Further research is being undertaken, and analysis broken down by socio-economic group may shed light on this contrary finding (personal communication Margaret Bentley).

Second, for nomadic pastoralists, the pattern of late dry season stress, documented for example by Gudrun Dahl for the Waso Borana in Kenya (Dahl, 1979:58–67), is not disputed. But a gloss on this has been the finding (White, 1986:19–20 and J. Swift, personal communication) that the most vulnerable and crucial time for pastoralists' herd management is often not the late dry season but the early rains. This is a time of change of climate and diet for animals, exposing them to diseases such as bloat, and also a time when cattle quite often calve. Bad luck or bad management at this time can be disastrous and conversely good luck or good management can increase stock numbers and quality.

Much of the professional excitement in the analysis of seasonal changes,

58

has been methodological. The approaches and methods of agro-ecosystem analysis (Conway, 1985a and b), rapid rural appraisal – RRA (Khon Kaen, 1987) and participatory rural appraisal – PRA (Mascarenhas *et al.*, 1991; Mascarenhas, 1992; Chambers, 1992a) have opened up new potentials in many aspects of rural development, including health and nutrition (*RRA Notes* 16). One of the most commonly used methods is seasonal diagramming.

Seasonal diagramming was developed in agro-ecosystem analysis and quickly proved its utility for presenting seasonal variations visually. Diagrams can show seasonal or more usually monthly changes in any condition or aspect of life, making it easy to see adverse linkages and to discuss remedies (for an Ethiopian example see ERCS 1988). With a shift from the data-extraction mode of RRA to the participatory mode of PRA, seasonal diagramming is now being carried out by rural people themselves, often drawing on the ground, and using stones, seeds and sticks as markers and counters to estimate for each month such aspects as days of rainfall and of labour, and to make monthly comparisons of conditions such as food availability, expenditure, income, and credit (Mascarenhas, 1992:15), and the incidence of diseases. The information shared can be of high quality, as with rainfall data presented by farmers in Nepal and compared with data from a nearby rainfall station (Gill, 1991b). In a PRA mode, seasonal analysis is conducted not by outsiders – Government or NGO staff – but by rural people themselves, and has proved popular among participants, and powerful as a means of sharing and analysing knowledge. With local variations, this has repeatedly confirmed the familiar scenario of the tropical rains as a lean and sick season.

The challenge to the medical and agricultural professions now is not just to come together to analyse and mitigate adverse seasonality, important and useful though that remains. It is to go further, by facilitating analysis by rural people themselves, empowering them to identify bad times, problems and opportunities. Rural people can then use their own diagrams and analysis to plan their own counterseasonal actions, and to make demands for appropriate and timely services and support.

59

5   Farmer-first: A Practical Paradigm for the Third Agriculture

> Probably the single most prevalent claim advanced by the proponents of a new paradigm is that they can solve the problems that have led the old one to a crisis . . .   T. Kuhn, *The Structure of Scientific Revolutions*

Three types of agriculture can be distinguished – industrial, green revolution, and a third, complex, diverse and risk-prone agriculture. For this third agriculture, supporting perhaps 1.4 billion people, the transfer-of-technology (TOT) paradigm of industrial and green revolution agriculture has not worked well. A better fit is found with the complementary farmer-first paradigm which is emerging. This entails reversals of explanation, learning, location and roles in agricultural research and extension. Baskets of choice for farmers replace packages of practices. It is farmers who analyse, choose, experiment and evaluate, while outsiders convene, catalyse, advise, search and supply, and provide support and consultancy. Extension is more lateral than vertical. Farming systems become more complex and diverse instead of simpler and more standard. Key challenges are to develop new modes of interaction for farmers, extensionists and scientists; to make better use of scarce extension and research resources; to spread participatory methods; and to establish farmer-first approaches in departments, institutes and universities. On meeting these challenges will depend the sustainable livelihoods of many millions of the poorest in the 1990s and into the 21st century.

The great challenge of the 1990s

With agricultural development and production on the one hand, and with poverty on the other, the 1970s and 1980s witnessed changes in reality and insight. By the mid-1980s, production had risen sharply in the industrial agriculture of the rich North, and in the green revolution (GR) agriculture of the well-watered fertile plains of the South; but it had risen much less in the complex, diverse and risk-prone (CDR) 'third' agriculture of the South, which is mainly rainfed, on undulating land, and found in hinterlands, mountains, hills, wetlands and the semi-arid, sub-humid and humid tropics. Food surpluses had depressed world prices, by creating a glut on the market. With the exception of Bangladesh, the other most populous agricultural countries of Asia – Burma, China, India, Indonesia, Pakistan, Philippines and Thailand – had either achieved food and foodgrain self-sufficiency or had got close to it (FAO, 1986). In contrast, for much of the third, non-GR agriculture of the South, there had been deepening crisis, with populations rising, land-holdings growing smaller, environments

60

degrading and per capita food production remaining static or declining. According to one estimate (Wolf, 1986), some 1.4 billion people were dependent on CDR agriculture, with roughly 100 million in Latin America, 300 million in Africa, and 1 billion in Asia; and short of an AIDS or similar pandemic or disaster, these were also the areas and countries where population growth rates would continue to be highest.

In the early 1990s world food surpluses are less, and populations continue to rise throughout the South, but the insights of the 1980s hold: it is

Table 5.1: Three types of agriculture summarized

Type of agriculture	Industrial	Green revolution	Third 'CDR'
P L A C E Main locations	Industrialized countries, plantations in the South	Irrigated and high rainfall, high potential areas in the South	Rainfed tropics, hinterlands, most of sub-Saharan Africa, etc.
Climatic zone	Temperate	Mainly tropical	Mainly tropical
S T A T U S Condition	Overdeveloped	Developed	Underdeveloped
Current production to sustainable production ratio	Far too high	Often near the limit	Low
Priority for production	Reduce production	Maintain production	Raise production
C H A R A C T E R Topography usually	Flat or undulating	Flat	Undulating
Farming system, relatively	Simple	Simple	Complex
Environment relatively	Uniform	Uniform	Diverse
Relative stability	Low risk	Low risk	High risk
Use of external inputs	Very High	High	Low
R & D Similarity of farmers' and research station conditions	High	High	Low
P R O B L E M S Farmers consulted about research priorities	Richer farmers sometimes	Richer farmers sometimes	Rarely
Number of scientists/ extensionists per farming system	More	More	Fewer

CDR = Complex, diverse, risk-prone

still true that the problem is less one of producing enough food in the world and more one of who grows it, where it is grown, and who has access to it. With population growth and environmental fragility in CDR areas, the problem is also one of generating sustainable livelihoods for the much larger populations of the future, and enabling most people to live adequately and decently where they are (Conroy and Litvinoff, 1988). The alternative is that they have to migrate, often in desperation, to GR and urban areas, where they depress wages and the incomes of other poor people, or to fragile mountain, forest or semi-arid environments where insecure tenure and other factors may deny sustainable livelihoods.

One great challenge for the 1990s is, then, to enable the third, CDR agriculture to transform itself into more sustainable and productive systems, and to support many more people. To be sure, maintaining production and tackling poverty in GR areas is also vital. But the problems and solutions there are better known, although changing (Byerlee, 1987) and have received more attention. Moreover, the normal professionalism of agricultural science has served those areas better, but fits badly with the needs and priorities of the third agriculture (Table 5.1).

Normal professionalism, transfer-of-technology and the third agriculture
Normal professionalism means the thinking, concepts, values and methods dominant in a profession. It is usually conservative, heavily defended, and reproduced through teaching, training, textbooks, professional rewards, and international professional meetings. Most professional mindsets change only slowly, sometimes long after the realities and priorities have changed. This is true in the social sciences as well as in the physical and biological sciences.

In agricultural research and extension, worldwide, the normal professional paradigm can be described as 'transfer-of-technology' or TOT (Chambers and Ghildyal, 1985). In this model, agricultural research priorities are determined by scientists and by funding agencies; scientists then experiment in-laboratory and on-station to generate new technology; and this is then handed over to extension for transfer to farmers. There have been many modifications and variants, but the TOT model is deeply embedded in normal professional thinking and prescription. It is reflected in teaching, in behaviour in the field, and in the rhetoric of development.

The TOT mode has served industrial and GR agriculture rather well. Physical and economic conditions on research stations have been similar to those of resource-rich farms and farm families, which are typical of these two types of agriculture (Tables 5.2 and 5.3). The reductionism of normal agronomic research, in which only a few variables are manipulated, has led to simple packages suitable for uniform controlled environments: E (the environment) has been made to fit high-yielding G (the genotype). Packages have served to standardize farming systems, and have fitted in with economies of scale associated with mechanization and subsidy. The outcome has been the well-known increases in productivity per unit of land in both industrial and GR agriculture.

However, the TOT model has not done well with the third agriculture. There have been limited successes, but no great production breakthroughs

Table 5.2: Typical contrasts in physical conditions

	Research experiment station	Resource-rich farm (RRF)	Resource-poor farm (RPF)
Topography	flat or sometimes terraced	flat or sometimes terraced	often undulating and sloping
Soils	deep, fertile, few constraints	deep, fertile, few constraints	shallow, infertile, often severe constraints
Macro and micro-nutrient deficiency	rare, remediable	occasional	quite common
Plot size and nature	large, square	large	small, irregular
Hazards	nil or few	few, usually controllable	more common – floods, droughts, animals grazing crops, etc.
Irrigation	usually available	often available	often non-existent
Size of management unit	large, contiguous	large or medium, contiguous	small, often scattered and fragmented
Natural vegetation	eliminated	eliminated or highly controlled	used or controlled at microlevel

Source: Chambers and Jiggins, 1986.

comparable to the Green Revolutions with wheat, maize and rice. The explanation lies partly in the contrasts between physical and economic conditions on research stations which are similar to those of resource rich farms and areas, and those of the resource-poor farms and farm families which are typical of CDR conditions (Tables 5.2 and 5.3). It also lies in the disjuncture between the nature of CDR agriculture on the one hand, and the nature of normal professionalism on the other. This can be appreciated by examining CDR agriculture in more detail.

The complexity and diversity of CDR farming systems have many aspects. Seven dimensions typically stand out:

Human The composition of households, their social structure and organisation, their labour power and activities, their stages in the domestic cycle, and their resources and access, vary within any one farming system, and can range from isolated and poor female-headed households with dependent children to large extended families with strong labour power.

Physical Typically, CDR farm holdings comprise sloping lands with a variety of conditions of soil, slope, shade, aspect and water supply. Micro-environments, including home gardens, are significant. Lands in different ecological zones are quite often part of the same holding.

Table 5.3: Typical contrasts in social and economic conditions

	Research experiment station	Resource-rich farm family	Resource-poor farm family
Access to seeds, fertilisers, pesticides and other purchased inputs	unlimited, reliable	high, reliable	low, unreliable
Source of seeds	foundation stocks and breeders' seed, high quality	purchased, high quality	own seeds
Access to credit when needed	unlimited	good access	poor access and seasonal shortages of cash when most needed
Irrigation, where facilities exist	fully controlled by research station	controlled by farmers or by others on whom s/he can rely	controlled by others, less reliable
Labour	unlimited, no constraint	hired, few constraints	family, constraining at seasonal peaks
Prices	irrelevant	lower than RPF for inputs. Higher than RPF for outputs	higher than RRF for inputs. Lower than RRF for outputs
Priority for food production	neutral	low	high
Access to extension services	good but one-sided	good, almost all material designed for this category	poor access; little relevant material

Source: Chambers and Jiggins, 1986.

Internal linkages In their internal linkages, CDR farming systems typically involve and rely on multiple and sequential interactions between crops, livestock, grasses, trees, and sometimes fish and insects. Intercropping and agroforestry in their many forms are typical of this sort of complexity.

External linkages Energy and nutrient linkages with external common property resources are typically important. These include firewood, wild foods, pasture and fodder. CPRs are often a vital source of nutrients, as where fodder leaves are carried from forests, or where livestock graze common land by day, in both cases generating farmyard manure to maintain fertility. A host of other 'minor' products are used by those who live near forests.

Temporal variations CDR farming systems have sharp seasonal dimensions, and differ according to conditions year by year. Different processes and activities are undertaken by different household members at at different times of the year, and depending on conditions, in different years.

Multiple enterprises CDR farming systems entail several or many enterprises. Many species of useful plants and animals are husbanded, and often these are multipurpose and multi-product. Off-farm activities and incomes are frequently significant for the farm household economy.

Risk CDR farming systems are risk-prone, subject to vagaries of climate, market access and prices, sickness, and social and physical disasters, and CDR farmers are risk-averse. Normal agricultural science does not fit well with this complexity, diversity and risk-aversion.

Complexity is sought by CDR farmers. As with natural ecosystems, internal agro-ecosystem and farming system complexity contributes to resilience, and reduces risk. But the complexity of CDR agriculture presents interactions which are difficult for scientists to study, multiply or enhance. Some lie in the gaps between dominant disciplines (concerning agroforestry, tree fodders, crop residues, biological energy use, etc.): normal science homes in on its primary and visible concerns – crops for agronomists, livestock for animal scientists, trees for foresters – rather than their 'secondary' and less visible linkages. Others are found in the creation and management of microenvironments which concentrate and conserve soil, water and nutrients, but which normal science usually overlooks (Chambers, 1990). Some opportunities lie in multiple simultaneous innovation and sequential management where several factors must be changed at the same time and then modified and managed adaptively. Examples are developing rainfed rice-fish farming, harvesting soils, nutrients or water, introducing a cover crop to inhibit weed growth, and agroforestry where there are tree-crop, tree-livestock or tree-crop-livestock interactions. For normal scientists tied to the inflexible reductionism of preset experimental design, these complexities can be unmanageable; and if scientists simplify for the sake of measurement, they cut out the very complexities which are the systems' strength.

Diversity compounds the misfit between normal science and CDR agriculture. CDR agriculture often presents many different farming systems within short distances, corresponding with differences which are ecological, such as altitude, rainfall, topography and soils, and social and economic, such as land tenure, farm size, social group, and access to services and markets. This raises questions of cost-effectiveness of research and of scientists' motivation when using normal R and D methods in the TOT mode. Any new variety or practice is likely to fit the conditions and needs of fewer farm families in CDR areas than in GR areas which are, or can be made, so much more uniform. Returns to research are then low because its total impact, even if successful, is small. This makes work harder to justify economically. It also reduces the prestige and incentives of CDR work for scientists looking for bigger breakthroughs.

65

Risk-aversion presents a third misfit. Normal TOT seeks to simplify and standardize, and stresses purchased inputs; but for CDR farmers, these add to risk. They, in contrast, often seek to reduce risk by complicating and diversifying their farming systems, and by relying on factors of production which are under their control.

These misfits are aggravated by the presence of fewer scientists per farming system in CDR than in GR agriculture (Chambers and Jiggins, 1986). The small number of scientists reflects the past unpopularity of work on CDR agriculture, its low status and its low political priority. Irrigated green revolution agriculture has understandably been preferred by scientists and PhD students for reasons which include accessibility, ease of control, and the assurance that experiments will generate acceptable research papers and PhD theses (Gupta, 1987).

Precisely the bad fit of normal professionalism with complexity, diversity and risk-aversion has served to conceal the potential of CDR agriculture. When the simple packages generated in the TOT mode have not been adopted, the conclusion has been drawn that the CDR areas lack potential. And even when a new crop variety or a new practice is adopted, it has tended to be on a small scale. So CDR areas are often referred to as 'resource-poor' or 'low-resource'.

A contrary case has been made out that the sustainable potential of CDR agriculture is considerable when assessed as a multiple of present performance (Bunch, 1987a; Chambers, 1987; Conroy and Litvinoff, 1988). A new literature based on experience with complicating, diversifying and intensifying CDR agriculture and gardening presents a rich array of practical options, many of them labour-intensive (see e.g. *ILEIA Newsletter* 1985– ; Mollison, 1990; Cheatle and Njoroge, 1991; Cleveland and Soleri, 1991; Reijntjes, Haverkort and Waters-Bayer, 1992). Labour availability may be a condition for their adoption, giving 'population pressure' a positive aspect. For example, recent research by a team from ODI and the University of Nairobi in Machakos District, Kenya, has found that a five-fold increase in population, from 250,000 in the 1930s to 1,250,000 in 1990 has been associated with an intensification of agriculture, an increase in tree cover, and a decline in soil erosion (ODI, 1991–); in short, that with rising population density there has evolved an agriculture which is more sustainable as well as more productive. The very diversity of CDR agriculture makes generalization from cases like this itself risk-prone. Nevertheless, evidence is accumulating that while for much GR agriculture, present production is close to its sustainable limit, for much CDR agriculture, present production is far below its sustainable potential.

Farmer first: the complementary paradigm

In seeking to serve farmers in achieving more of that potential, the TOT paradigm is in crisis. There have been successes; but compared with industrial and green revolution agriculture, TOT has not done well. Research priorities and locations have often been wrong, messages have been misfits, and packages have been rejected. Historically, (Table 5.4) non-adoption of

66

Table 5.4: Research and extension: beliefs, and socio-economic research frontiers 1950–2000

	Explanation of farmers' non-adoption	Prescription	Key extension activity	Socio-economic research frontiers	Dominant research methods
1950s 1960s	Ignorance	Extension	Teaching	Understanding the diffusion and adoption of technology	Questionnaire surveys
1970s 1980s	Farm-level constraints	Remove constraints	Supplying inputs	Understanding farming systems	Constraints analysis; Farming systems research
1990s	Technology does not fit	Change the process	Facilitating farmer participation	Enhancing farmers' competence. Understanding and changing professional behaviour	Participatory research by and with farmers

recommendations has been attributed first to farmers' ignorance, to be overcome through more and better extension, and then to farm-level constraints, with the solution in easing the constraints to make the farm more like the research station. For CDR agriculture, these explanations have now been found largely wanting: farmers are far more knowledgeable and better informed than agricultural professionals used to suppose; and farming conditions are, and will remain, different from those of the research station.

So the crisis has led to questioning the very processes which generate agricultural technology, and to the exploration of new approaches. Increasingly during the 1980s, innovators in the agricultural and social sciences worked with CDR farmers to find solutions to these problems. By concentrating on what they found to work, they evolved a new paradigm for agricultural research and extension. The approaches of this paradigm have been given various labels: farmer-back-to-farmer (Rhoades and Booth, 1982); farmer-first-and-last (Chambers and Ghildyal, 1985); farmer participatory research – FPR (Farrington and Martin, 1987); Participatory Technology Development – PTD (ILEIA, 1989); and Approach Development (Scheuermeier n.d.). The different names conceal a commonality: in all these approaches, farmers' priorities and participation are key. For inclusiveness and brevity, I shall use the term farmer-first (FF) to describe this family of approaches (see also Lightfoot et al., 1989; Chambers, Pacey and Thrupp, 1989).

There are now many published sources on FF and related experience. ODI has published (Amanor, 1989) a bibliography of 340 items on farmer participatory research. Any selection will miss much, but a short list can include *Experimental Agriculture* (Farrington, 1988); papers of the Agricultural Administration (Research and Extension) Network of ODI; the work of Jacqueline Ashby and her colleagues at CIAT in Colombia (Ashby *et al.*, 1987; Ashby, 1990; Quiros *et al.*, 1991), of Roland Bunch and World Neighbors (Bunch, 1985; Gubbels, 1988), of D.M. Maurya (1988) and others involved in farming systems research in Eastern India, of David Norman and colleagues in Botswana (1988), of Robert Rhoades and others at CIP in Peru (Rhoades, 1982) and in the Philippines (Rhoades *et al.*, 1990), of Sumberg and Okali (1988) on alley farming in Nigeria, and of Baker and others in Brazil (1988). In Southeast Asia, examples of FF and of movements in its direction include SUAN (the Southeast Universities' Agroecosystems Network); agro-ecosystem analysis (Conway, 1985, 1986); the pioneering of rapid rural appraisal (RRA) by the University of Khon Kaen in Thailand (Khon Kaen University, 1987; Lovelace, Subhadira and Simaraks, 1988); the work of the Northeast Rainfed Agriculture Development Project (NERAD), also in Thailand; and the innovations of the Farming Systems Development Project, Eastern Visayas, in the Philippines (Lightfoot *et al.*, 1988; Repulda *et al.*, 1987; Tung and Balina, 1988).

The essence of FF is reversals of parts of TOT that have tended to go unquestioned. A reversal of explanation looks for reasons why farmers do not adopt new technology not in the ignorance of the farmer but in defi-

Table 5.5: Transfer-of-technology and farmer-first compared

	TOT	FF
Main objective	Transfer technology	Empower farmers
Analysis of needs and priorities by outsiders	Outsiders	Farmers facilitated by outsiders
Transferred by outsiders to farmers	Precepts Messages Package of practices	Principles Methods Basket of choices
The 'menu'	Fixed	A la carte
Farmers' behaviour	Hear messages Act on precepts Adopt, adapt or reject package	Use methods Apply principles Choose from basket and experiment
Outsiders' desired outcomes emphasize	Widespread adoption of package	Wider choices for farmers Farmers' enhanced adaptability
Main mode of extension	Agent-to-farmer	Farmer-to-farmer
Roles of extension agent	Teacher Trainer	Facilitator Searcher for and provider of choice

ciencies in the technology and the process that generated it. A reversal of learning has researchers and extension workers learning from farmers. Location and roles are also reversed, with farms and farmers central instead of research stations, laboratories and scientists.

In this framework, much of the earlier farming systems research can be seen as an extension of TOT: information was obtained from farmers by outsider professionals, and taken away by them to analyse and decide what would be good for the farmers, and what experiments should be designed and executed. In contrast, FF reverses roles. Analysis, choice and experimentation are conducted with and by farmers themselves, with outsider professionals in a catalytic, facilitating and support role.

In the late 1980s, FF methods were evolving fast. The importance of learning farmers' priorities, and putting them first, was increasingly recognised. The question was how to do it. Different methods and variants of methods were tried. Some of the contrasts with TOT are presented in Table 5.4. While not all of these are found all the time, and some can be followed without others, they are mutually reinforcing and cohere as a paradigm contrasting with and complementary to TOT. Farmer participation is a widespread and crucial element. FF also goes beyond field participation to influence decisions and methods for on-station research.

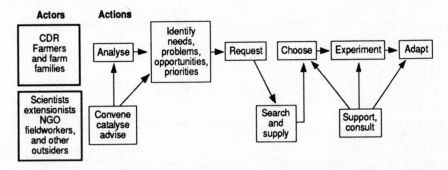

Figure 5.1: *Activities in the farmers' analysis-choice-experiment approach*

In the early 1990s the frontiers continue to move. There is renewed attention (e.g. Scoones and Thompson, 1992) to questions of whose knowledge counts – that of scientists or that of farmers. Knowledge and priorities vary – both within communities, differing for individuals, groups and genders, and between rural people and outsider professionals. The interactions between outsider professionals and rural people have become a focus, paralleling the priority given to outsiders' behaviour and attitudes in participatory rural appraisal (PRA) (Mascarenhas *et al.*, 1991; Shah, 1991).

Beyond this, the question has become whose analysis counts, and how analysis by farmers, and especially by female and resource-poor farmers, can be supported and strengthened.

Farmer participation can and should be locally developed and adapted (Heinrich *et al.*, 1991:13), take various forms and not be blueprinted. How-

69

ever, one sequence can be described in order to present some of the changes in roles which are involved. This is an iterative process of farmers' analysis, choice, and experiment followed by evaluation and extension. The main activities of farmers and roles of outsiders are:

Farmers' activities	*New roles for outsiders*
Analysis	Convenor, catalyst, adviser
Choice	Searcher and supplier
Experiment	Supporter and consultant

The actors and activities are presented diagrammatically in Figure 5.1. Let us consider these main activities in turn.

Analysis

This exploits farmers' comparative advantage in knowledge. Farmers are experts on their farming systems. Their analysis, if done well, can be expected automatically to screen out impractical irrelevances with a speed and accuracy to which no outsider could aspire, and should home in on their needs. In the process, farmers identify their priorities according to their own criteria. Outsiders can contribute by convening groups, encouraging observation, asking key starter questions, and facilitating participatory mapping and diagramming by farmers in support of farmers' own analysis.

Farmers' analysis has been promoted and supported in many ways:

- Sequences of farmers' group discussions and visits (Norman *et al.*, 1988; Baker *et al.*, 1988; Lightfoot *et al.*, 1988)
- Observation, inspection and discussion – systematic observation of innovations by farmers (Shah *et al.*, 1991); visiting other farmers, research stations, or trial sites (Ashby, *et al.*, 1987)
- Innovator workshops, where farmer innovators meet and discuss and compare their new practices (Ashby *et al.*, 1987; Abedin and Haque, 1989)
- The use of key priming questions by outsiders, such as 'What would an ideal variety look like to you?', 'What would you like your landscape to look like in the future?', 'What do you farmers talk about when you get together?', 'Why do other farmers have different practices to you?', and the unhurried sequence 'What was farming like when you were young, how has it changed, what problems have you faced, how have you tried to tackle them, and with what results?'

One of the most promising developments has been visual sharing and analysis through diagrams (*RRA Notes*, 1988– *passim*; Conway, 1989; Gupta *et al.*, 1989; Mascarenhas, 1992). Initially these were thought of largely as diagrams which outsider professionals would draw and then share with farmers, or which rural people would draw, revealing to outsiders how they saw things.

In the early 1990s developments have been quite dramatic as it it has become evident that rural people have a greater ability to make and analyse their own diagrams than had been supposed. These diagrams include resource maps, social maps, census and health maps, and farm maps (Mascarenhas and Kumar, 1991); seasonal diagrams; trend and change analysis; matrix scoring and ranking for varieties of a crop (ICRISAT, 1991), tree, weed, animal, or fish, for methods for soil conservation, for sources of credit and inputs, and so on; and causal and flow diagramming of farming systems (Lightfoot, Feldman and Abedin, 1991; Lightfoot, Noble and Morales, 1991; Guijt and Pretty, 1992).

One method developed in India and Botswana in 1992 is matrix scoring for a 'wish' variety of a crop. Women or men farmers identify crop varieties which are important to them, and their criteria of assessment (early maturing, high yield, drought-tolerant, good for fodder etc) are elicited. On the ground or on paper, they draw a matrix with the varieties on one axis and the criteria on the other. They then use seeds or other counters to score each box. After this, they are given a fixed number of seeds and asked to allocate these for the characteristics of a 'wish' variety that they would like scientists or extensionists to provide for them. When this method was used in Botswana in June 1992, a senior scientist observed that farmers had more criteria than scientists, that some criteria differed, and that scientists could respond to the priorities expressed by the farmers.

Search
Participatory analysis, as in this Botswana example, can express priorities and generate requests for varieties or for information. CDR farmers want and need choice to enhance adaptability. The role of the outsider, whether researcher or extension agent, is then to look for and supply a range of genetic material and a range of information about practices and potentials. An example from the Philippines is a research agenda geared towards meeting farmers' needs which included search for alternative live mulch, alternative leguminous trees, and alternative sources of leguminous cover crops (FARMIIS, 1987). The demand here is not for the package of practices of normal research and extension, but for a basket of choices.

Methodological questions refer especially to the organisation of extension and research. Extension information systems have to be stood on their head, passing requests up first, before messages down. The difficulty of this reversal can be inferred from experience in the Philippines. Of seven management information systems for agriculture and natural resources reported (Valmayor and Mamon, 1987), six (for research management information, equipment infrastructure management, manpower management, financial management, publications mailing, and administrative support) appear designed to serve central management rather than farmers' needs for information. The seventh – a Research Information Storage and Retrieval System – with potential use to provide information and choices to farmers, was described only in the future tense, with the statement that financial support was needed to extend it to regions, suggesting that it was not yet in operation. As here, information systems normally serve the managers at the centre before farmers at the periphery.

71

Choice
Presenting choice to farmers can take several forms:

- Minikits (a well-known and well-established approach), containing several varieties of a crop, and several fertilizers, for farmers to test and choose from on their own
- 'Wait-and-see and pick-and-choose' (personal communication Diane Rocheleau). Planting a range of species, varieties or lines and giving farmers an opportunity to observe them and choose from them
- Releasing small batches of advanced breeders' lines matched to the characteristics of farmers' landraces (Maurya *et al.*, 1988)
- Pre-screening of varietal materials by farmers, as with bush beans and cassava at CIAT in Colombia (Ashby *et al.*, 1987)
- Presenting farmers with alternatives for research and facilitating their choice of research priorities (Lightfoot, Axinn and Singh, 1991)

There are methodological questions about how best to elicit and support farmers' choices. More and more, group discussion and analysis is becoming the mode. In Colombia, for example, difficulty was experienced with individual farmers making selections from 35 superficially similar varieties of snap beans; but as a group, farmers did better. They walked through rows of beans, examining bean plants and pods of each variety separately. Research staff asked them to indicate which varieties they considered should continue to be tested and which not. Farmers' discussion rapidly focused on quality characteristics related to market acceptability. In about an hour farmers identified two climbing varieties and two bush varieties which they considered outstanding by their criteria and six bush varieties they would test further (Ashby *et al.*, 1987). It may well be generally true, as in this example, that groups can analyse better than individuals.

Experimentation
Typically farmers are themselves continuously experimenting, adapting technology, and learning from observations and experience (Johnson, 1972; Richards, 1985; Rhoades, 1987, 1989). Working out how to work with them as experimenting colleagues is a challenge to scientists and extensionists.

What is shared with farmers is, in a collaborative and facilitating mode, not so much packages and precepts as:

(i)   choices of genetic material and of practices;
(ii) methods; and
(iii) principles.

Farmers have their own ways of trying out genetic material and practices. Methods of small-scale experimentation can be taught to them, as recommended by Roland Bunch (1985:138–46) as part of the successful World Neighbours approach. Working out how to work with farmers as experimenters is a challenge to scientists and extensionists; mistakes are easy to make, and much can be learnt about approach and methods from honest accounts of difficulties as well as successes, such as that of Jeffrey

72

Bentley and Werner Melara (1991) concerning their experiences 'Experimenting with Honduran Farmer-Experimenters'.

Some of the most successful transfers may be of principles, rather than practices. A famous example is the International Potato Centre's experience with diffused light storage in potatoes. Farmers themselves discovered that sprouting in storage, a problem with new varieties, was inhibited by diffused light storage. Scientists learned from the farmers, and transferred the principle internationally. But there was no standard store to be built; farm families did not adopt a design but applied a principle, in a myriad of locally adapted different ways.

Many methodological questions remain. One persistent problem is allowing and enabling farmers to 'own' their experiments, and not to be dominated by outsiders. Farmer-designed and farmer managed trials are part of the rhetoric of on-farm research, if still rarely the reality. Enhancing farmers' capacity to experiment remains a frontier on which progress is needed and can be expected.

Evaluation and extension
In the FF mode, evaluation is not by scientists' peers but by farmers' adoption. For D.M. Maurya (personal communication), whether a line justifies the bulking of seed depends on whether the farmers who try it are asked for seed by other farmers. With farmers' inspections of one anothers' fields and trials, evaluation and extension merge. Extension is not top-down, as often in the T and V mode in practice, but lateral, from farmer to farmer, as with peanuts after rice in northeast Thailand (Jintrawet *et al.*, 1985), with soil erosion control in the Philippines (S. Fujisaka personal communication) and in the approach of World Neighbors (Bunch, 1985). Farmers are often the best extension agents, and the best facilitators of analysis, choice and experimentation by other farmers.

The FF paradigm is still evolving and will never have a final shape, since it is organic rather than a structure. All the same, recurring elements hang together and support each other. One is the resonance between enhancing the adaptability of farmers through widening their choice and knowledge, and enhancing the adaptability of outsiders – scientists, extensionists and NGO staff – through widening theirs. For farmers, the choices are of practices and plants; for outsiders, of behaviour, approaches and methods. For farmers, the adaptability is to uncertain climatic and economic conditions; for outsiders it is to needs, opportunities and insights as they arise. For all, decentralization and reversals of authority to those 'below' are entailed: to empower farmers to analyse, choose, experiment and evaluate; and to empower outsiders, however junior, to use their initiative and choose methods that that are fitting for local conditions.

FF thus has its own style, which is decentralized and democratic, with mutual respect and service between outsiders and farmers. Personality is a key variable here. FACE (Farmers Analyse, Choose, Experiment) may not be a felicitous acronym, but it can serve to underline the crucial importance of the quality of the face-to-face interactions of farmers and outsiders. A personal impression is that those who have succeeded in pioneering FF

73

approaches have been sympathetic people who empathize with farmers and respect and like them. This cannot be expected of all outsiders, but the fascination and psychic rewards of working closely with farmers and learning from and with them are so high, that more and more outsiders may be attracted to this mode.

Challenges for the future

The argument for the FF paradigm to complement TOT has been developed here in terms of the third, CDR, agriculture, but its application is not necessarily so limited. It may increasingly fit the trends in GR and industrial agriculture towards complexity and diversity. Some of the new GR complexity comes from the range of inputs (seed, fertilizer, pesticide) and associated practices that have become available and needed. Some also comes from the diversification of crops and sequences, for example with non-rice crops increasingly grown in a second season following rice in South and Southeast Asia, and with rotations such as rice-potato-wheat, cotton-wheat, and sugarcane-wheat. Further, the withdrawal or reduction of input subsidies in both GR and industrial agriculture may permit, encourage and even force increased on-farm diversification and complexity, as has happened in New Zealand. FF approaches and methods, devised and evolved to meet the special challenges of CDR agriculture, may in the 1990s be found to apply more and more in GR and industrial agriculture, helping the 1990s to become a decade, worldwide, of diversification.

For the present, though, the higher priority appears to lie in CDR agriculture, evolving and testing approaches and methods, and striving for cost-effectiveness, spread and sustainability. Four key challenges raised in this chapter can be sharpened with practical questions as follows:

Inventiveness
The challenge is for farmers, extensionists and scientists to find and develop new modes of interacting, new methods of analysis, choice, experimenting, and evaluation, and new ways of spreading and institutionalizing existing and new approaches and methods.

Can the necessary inventiveness be nurtured and rewarded through:

- training scientists and extensionists in relaxed, democratic behaviour, in lateral thinking, and in creativity;
- competitions for new approaches and methods, and awards for farmers, extensionists and scientists who invent them;
- field camps with methodological innovation as their aim?

Parsimony
The challenge is to make more sparing and effective use of the scarce resources of extension and agricultural research for the many complex, diverse and risk-prone farming systems.

Can better use be made of scarce extension and research resources by:

- convening farmers' groups which then analyse and act largely on their own;
- reorienting extension to facilitate farmers' analysis and experimentation, and to search for what farmers need;
- lateral transfer of methods by farmers, with farmers as facilitators;
- farmers' priorities learnt by agricultural scientists directly, face-to-face, in the field;
- farmers' evaluation of on-station research to assess priorities?

Spread
The challenge is to achieve rapid spread of new participatory methods and approaches.

Can spread be speeded by:

- newsletters, broadsheets, videos for farmers as well as for those in professional organizations;
- visits and exchanges;
- lateral spread by farmers and through farmers' organizations;
- publicising and spreading individual methods, such as participatory farm mapping, and 'wish' variety matrix scoring, as popular and powerful points of entry?

Embedding
The challenge is to gain acceptance of participation and FF as professional and operational norms in large bureaucratic organisations – departments of agricultural research, research institutes, departments of extension, training institutes, and agricultural universities.

Can FF be established in large bureaucratic institutions in the longer term through:

- interaction with innovative NGOs;
- articles in 'hard' journals;
- new textbooks;
- introducing FF approaches and methods into students' fieldwork?

The ultimate potential of the family of participatory approaches and methods described here as farmer-first is not yet knowable, but probably vast. How well and how fast that potential will be realized depends on the interplay of many factors, including the awareness, organization and actions of farmers themselves. Perhaps, though, at this stage, much of the opportunity lies with outsider professionals, many thousands of whom are already in a position to act. They have a heavy responsibility. Much hangs on their personal vision, creativity and courage. For, if the arguments of this chapter are correct, on their decisions and actions – what they do and do not do – will depend the livelihoods of many millions of the poorest in the 1990s and into the twenty-first century.

6 Normal Professionalism and the Early Project Process: Problems and Solutions

> The disturbing feature of most of these design and appraisal faults is that they are well-known, yet the evaluation literature is replete with complaints that they keep being repeated.
>
> Robert Cassen and Associates, *Does Aid Work?*

The early project process is dominated by engineers and economists, and preoccupations with infrastructure, budgets, schedules, and quantification. The way professionals and organizations think and operate biases the process against poor people. A new professionalism and a new paradigm start with people rather than things, and adaptive processes rather than blueprints. Practical implications for this approach include the need for calibre, commitment and continuity in field staff, restraint in funding, use of methods of rapid rural appraisal, and support for 'learning projects' without deadlines or targets.

Definitions and scope

In this chapter 'the early project process' refers in the sense of World Bank terminology to identification, preparation, analysis, and appraisal (Gittinger, 1982:21–4), and the equivalents to these activities as conducted by other governmental, aid and NGO agencies. This early project process presents many well-known and well-documented weaknesses. Those listed by Cassen and Associates in the quotation at the head of this chapter refer to aid, and include:

- overestimating the recipient's capacity for administration and implementation;
- imprecise forecasting of the effects on intended beneficiaries;
- neglect of maintenance and recurrent cost requirements for operation;
- lack of understanding of the human, social, and physical environment;
- lack of attention to relationships with other projects and programmes.

These are all important, and recent writing would add others, especially inadequate participation in all stages of the process by those intended to benefit (see e.g. Rondinelli, 1983; Korten and Klauss, 1984; Cernea, 1985; Uphoff, 1985). The thesis of this chapter is that these are not all; that to correct them , however necessary, is not sufficient and that in addition there are other factors and defects, which also partly explain why mistakes go on being repeated. These are associated with normal professionalism and with political and bureaucratic pressures. 'Normal professionalism' here means the thinking, values, methods and behaviour dominant in professions, disciplines and departments. In this chapter, it refers especially to

76

engineering and economics as the professions and disciplines most influential in defining and executing the early project process. The argument is that measures can be taken to mitigate or avoid these factors and defects once they have been recognised.

Normal professionalism

Normal professionalism has ingrained biases. These reflect 'core' or 'first' characteristics which contrast with others which are 'peripheral' or 'last' (see Table 1.1, and Chambers, 1983:171–9). These show up, to take one illustration, in preferences for technology, as in Table 6.1.

Table 6.1: Preferences for technology

Core or First	Peripheral or Last
large-scale	small-scale
capital-intensive	labour-intensive
inorganic	organic
market-linked	subsistence-linked
mechanical	human or animal-powered
developed in core	developed in periphery
'high' technology	'low' technology

The 'first' list is preferred by most normal professionals, while the 'last' list is usually closer to the resources and needs of poorer rural people.

There are many influences which reproduce and reinforce normal professionalism's bias against the poor. Some of these are evident in the relative status between and within professions and disciplines. High status, and the rewards of power and money that go with it, are associated with things more than people (or with people treated as things), with men more than women, with quantification more than qualitative assessment, and with specialization more than general competence. Precision with things and numbers is valued more than participation with people. Much normal professionalism values hard data, measurement, calculations, the correct execution of established rules of analysis, and planned blueprints which promise control and certainty. Urban concerns are also preferred to rural, and industrial to agricultural. Interlocking, these tendencies mean that engineering has higher status and carries more weight than agronomy, and economics than sociology or social anthropology.

Professions and the early project process

High normal professional status coincides with the professions and disciplines – engineering and economics – which are dominant in the early phases of the evolution of both institutions and projects.

With institutions, the outstanding example is the World Bank. Its original title – the International Bank for Reconstruction and Development – reflects the primacy of the physical in the word 'Reconstruction', which

77

moreover precedes 'Development'. The early concentration of the Bank on infrastructure and industry is strikingly illustrated by John King's (1967) book *Economic Development Projects and Their Appraisal* which presented 30 cases, of which 17 were in electric power, 9 in transport, and 4 in industry. None was classified as agricultural, or concerned with human resources. Given this emphasis, it was natural that the World Bank should be dominated by engineers and economists, as were aid agencies generally.

With projects, too, a similar 'natural' dominance is normal. Most projects of any size, even when they are agricultural, start with hardware and construction – roads, houses, stores, dams and so on – requiring surveys, planning, blueprints, procurement, purchasing, scheduling, and construction – all within the domain of engineers. These are preceded by financial estimates, economic assessments, and statistical justifications – the domain of economists. People, and the professions concerned with people, tend to come later. Although there have been changes since the days when Hamnett (1970) was recruited as a sociologist to solve the problems with people after the engineers had made the decisions about things, it is still true that in larger projects the 'harder' professions set the style and the main agenda. Sociologists and social anthropologists start as poor relations. They are rather a nuisance. Their contributions often appear negative. They often explain why things should not be done, or should be done more slowly. They raise objections and slow down disbursements and implementation. The view of the higher status and more powerful professionals can be that those concerned with people should keep quiet until their time comes – later.

The law of prior bias then operates. This is that what comes first in a process sets patterns and takes most. The modes of operation of the blueprinting phase of engineering design and economic assessment, dealing with physical things, planning and estimates, carry over into implementation and operation. The style has been set, and remains, top-down, timebound, and mechanistic. Thinking, values, methods and behaviour which fit and work with things are then applied later to people, with whom they fit and work less well.

Bureaucratic and political pressures

Bureaucratic and political dynamics also reinforce 'first' and prior biases. Aid officials and host country officials are subject to pressures which are so prevalent and well-known as to be commonplace. These are

- to produce a portfolio of projects quickly;
- to spend budgets, especially aid budgets, by deadlines;
- to include capital goods from donor countries as part of projects;
- to reduce staff numbers (as retrenching donor governments slim their aid agencies and host country bureaucracies are cut back in structural readjustment).

In aid agencies, these pressures favour fewer, larger projects with more 'first' characteristics, since these enable fewer aid staff to spend more, to spend it faster, and to spend more of it in the donor countries. Normal

78

professionalism is then reinforced and normal professionals rewarded. Engineers and economists are seen to have most to contribute to the expeditious implementation of such projects, while soft social scientists asking awkward questions complicate things and slow projects down. Engineers and economists remain on top. Those primarily concerned with people, especially the poorer people, remain marginal.

In many agencies, things have changed and continue to change. I do not undervalue the enormous professional contributions of engineers or economists, nor suggest that they always neglect people. The point I am making, though, is that there are systemic forces – in normal professionalism, in the sequence of activities in the project process, and in the dynamics of aid bureaucracy – which favour the 'first' and neglect the 'last'.

Project process pathology

The theory of project identification and of other early project activities is that they are subject to systematic and rigorous procedures. Enormous efforts have been made to develop and improve these, especially their mathematical components. In the real world, however, major defects remain, and separately or combined, reduce benefits to the poorer. Four are easily overlooked: irreversibility of commitment; anti-poor bias in methodology; the 'cooking' of cost-benefit analysis; and additive procedures.

Irreversibility of commitment
With medium and large donor-supported projects, commitment to go ahead is often irreversible at an early stage. Whatever the theory in the textbooks, in reality the decision is 'pre-empted' rather than 'taken' because of a slide of political commitment making it embarrassing for a donor to withdraw. This can occur long before the later stages of preparation, analysis and appraisal. It would be worth investigating whether it is true that the larger the project, the earlier the commitment becomes irreversible. 'Commitment' here refers not to any formal agreement or signing of documents, but to the point at which withdrawal becomes politically difficult to contemplate. There are cases, like the development of the New Lands in Egypt, or the railway to the North in Burkina Faso, where Governments have pressed ahead with little or no donor support; but more common are situations in which donors are hooked early on and then cannot escape even if they want to. Two examples from British aid are the announcement by the then Prime Minister, James Callaghan, on a visit to India, of a £30 million fertilizer aid project for which there had been no serious appraisal, and the Victoria dam in Sri Lanka, the largest British foreign aid project ever, where donors were in competition and so in a hurry to become committed. Whether these have proved good projects is not the point here. The point is that for political reasons, including in those days the need to spend the aid budget, commitment to go ahead was deep at an early stage, and largely independent of the formal project process which then followed.

The irreversibility of such commitments, whether by donors or by host governments, can even resist adverse technical reports. Commitment in Kenya to irrigation on the lower Tana was probably politically irreversible

79

for the Kenya Government as early as the mid-1960s, despite negative appraisals by a succession of technical missions. It gave birth to the Bura Irrigation Project which must be a leading contender for the strongly contested prize for the least economic irrigation scheme in sub-Saharan Africa; and not only is the project grossly uneconomic, but those who were meant to benefit have, despite huge costs, done badly (Moris, 1987:103–6). Bad projects rarely benefit the poor in the long term; and preventing them requires early action to slow or stop the slide into commitment.

The anti-poor bias in methodology
Among the many biases in normal professionalism, those which are methodological are among the least recognised. In project identification, the most important events usually occur in the early stages, but methodologically these are the least determinate, the least observed, and the least written about. For these reasons, identification in the narrow sense of having and lodging the idea of a project is often, *ex post*, a black box. And *ex ante* it is easily influenced by those with special interests or local power. The neglect of the identification phase is illustrated in J. Price Gittinger's classic and magisterial *Economic Analysis of Agricultural Projects* (1982), which devotes only one page out of 443 (not including the bibliography and glossary-index) to 'Identification'. To be fair, one page of Gittinger contains more words than most books. It is, though, the content as well as the length of the treatment that matters. The page starts:

> The first stage in the (project) cycle is to find potential projects. There are many, many sources from which suggestions may come. The most common will be well-informed technical specialists and local leaders. While performing their professional duties, technical specialists will have identified many areas where they feel new investment might be profitable. Local leaders will generally have a number of suggestions about where investment might be carried out . . . (*ibid.*: 21)

Other sources of suggestions include proposals to extend existing programmes, and needs for certain agricultural products. For all these, though, Gittinger says little about the process and procedures. These are, it seems, most commonly left open to the normal biases of professionals and to the suggestions of the members of local elites. Such an approach appears unlikely to generate many projects which give priority to the expressed needs and priorities of the poorer rural people.

The 'home economics' of cost-benefit analysis
Such biases in identification are liable to be confirmed by early irreversible commitment. But in theory they should be mitigated by cost-benefit analysis (CBA).

Certainly, in choosing between alternatives for components of a project, CBA is useful. Sensitivity analysis is a useful aid to decisionmaking. Economic analysis can be used effectively for damage limitation (Harvey, 1986:448–50). It can also be used to prevent bad projects if they can be caught early enough.

80

But the defects of CBA are several. Partly it is the seductive attraction of the single number – a benefit-cost ratio, or an internal rate of return – which is easily given more weight than it deserves; Gittinger himself warns that economic and financial measures are only tools of decisionmaking and not substitutes for judgement. Partly it is that discounting the future supports decisions which are unsound for the environment and for future generations. Especially where future livelihoods are likely to be more vulnerable, and people likely to be poorer, there is a case for discounting in reverse, valuing the future more, not less, than the present. Partly, too, CBA has difficulty accounting for losers from development projects, and often they are the poorer, and unseen and unheard.

Finally, CBA appears to be what it is rarely, if at all: an objective scientific procedure impartially carried out. For in its practice it is more art than science, and grey art at that. Irreversibility of commitment, political pressures, and personal judgements of the worth of a project, combine to encourage and legitimate a practice unlikely to feature in textbooks, manuals, or courses such as those of the Economic Development Institute of the World Bank. This is working cost-benefit analysis backwards, a skill transmitted, one may surmise through craft apprenticeship in economists' offices, or reinvented under stress. In this reversed process, a judgement is first made about what Internal Rate of Return (IRR) is appropriate, and then assumptions – about future prices, rates of implementation, rates of adoption of practices by farmers and so on – are derived so as to generate the IRR required. The judgement on which the IRR was first assessed may have been sound. It may also have been politically determined. When political commitment is already irreversible, and a certain IRR is needed for a project to be accepted bureaucratically, then not to follow such a practice of 'cooking' may combine political embarrassment and conflict with dismal prospects for the analyst's career. It may even be that the larger and more expensive the project, the more the IRR is likely to be an artefact of political realities, the hypothesis being that the bigger the cake, the more thorough the cooking.

Additive procedures

One response to defects and criticisms such as these has been to reorganize and add to the procedures of the early project process. In this USAID has been in the lead. New appraisal criteria have been agreed and incorporated in required procedures. At first sight these look good. USAID's social soundness analysis, for example, raises questions about people which could otherwise be overlooked. But the succession of additional considerations – who gains and who loses, women, and now the environment – contrasts and conflicts with cutbacks in aid agency staff. When fewer people have to do more they either work harder, put the work out, change their methods, take longer, or do less and do it worse. The last is the greatest danger. Just as adding another member to a multidisciplinary team can reduce communication in the team, so adding another criterion or procedure in the early project stages can lead to superficiality and tokenism on the part of those who are overworked. It can then appear more important to be able to show that, say, women's interests have been investigated and reported on, than that the report on women's interests is correct and has actually been acted upon. Adverse reports, unless aid agencies have staff with time, capacity and authority to act on them, are liable to culminate as entries in files which show that the required study was completed and the report duly received. Consummation is then confined to a tick in a box. With procedures, it is but a short step from the complex to the cosmetic.

Large projects: prevention often better than cure

These four defects – irreversibility of commitment, the anti-poor bias in methodology, the cooking of cost-benefit analysis, and additive procedures – bear on the strategic question of choice of size of project.

The current fashion of condemning large projects can go too far. It is true that large projects are sought after by host governments and donors alike for well-known less than altruistic reasons such as prestige, patronage, personal ambition, commercial interests, corruption and the need to expend budgets. But such motives should be separated from the question whether a project is or was worth doing. Critics of existing large projects in the rural sector, such as big dams, hydroelectric schemes, major road construction, and processing factories, should reflect, case by case, on whether they are saying that a given project could and should have been implemented better, or that it should not have been done at all. Faced with the latter question, negative social scientists will sometimes crumble. Each case, *ex ante* as well as *ex post*, deserves to be examined on its merits. A final argument in favour of large projects could be that with understaffed aid agencies, the lower administrative demands made in total by fewer larger projects would improve the chances that the additive procedures designed to protect and favour the poor, women, and the environment would be well implemented and would bite.

That said, much evidence and argument makes large projects look less attractive than in the past. They have always been vulnerable to major and expensive problems. When Albert Hirschman in the 1960s studied 11 large World Bank projects, he feared a biased sample because of the high standards insisted on by the Bank, but reported 'Fortunately, (at least for my research) I found, upon looking more closely, that not one of the projects I had selected had been free from serious problems' (1967:1). Nor was the 'creativity' he found being mustered to overcome problems costless. Two decades later, many of the better big projects have already been identified and implemented. Those that remain are less attractive, riskier, and on worse sites, and often involve more losers in populations that would be harmed or displaced. Adverse environmental effects are also better understood and more predictable. To these points can now be added the first three defects discussed above – irreversibility of commitment, the anti-poor bias in methodology, and the misuse of cost-benefit analysis. Big is not always or necessarily bad. But it is now more often bad than it used to be.

In consequence, we are moving into a phase in which self-restraint and new skills are increasingly needed to question large projects and seek alternatives to them. How to do this is a subject for research, public information, and lobbying. One of the healthiest developments of recent years has been the emergence of international networks of activist NGOs committed to the rights of peripheral people who stand to lose from projects. Another has been the tough line taken within and by the World Bank over the rights and welfare of poor people displaced by dams, to the extent that this has been effective. But there still remain questions of how host and donor agencies, staff and politicians can learn to prevent and abstain from bad large projects. This subject deserves study in its own right. For the present, four suggestions are:

(i)   to identify and count the losers from a project and give their welfare a high weighting;
(ii) to seek ways to break large projects into smaller units. This is more often possible than realised. For example, several small dams along a river, with lift irrigation from their reservoirs, can quite often substitute for one large dam with gravity irrigation;
(iii) to avoid premature political commitment by keeping a low profile, emphasising political risks and costs, and avoiding early high-level meetings of donor and host political leaders;
(iv) to prefer consultants who are willing and able to give a proposal the thumbs down, and reward major negative decisions with public recognition (a place in the honours list for recommending *against* the big dam and so losing the lucrative contract for supervising implementation).

The new paradigm and the new professionalism

The prevention of bad big projects can be compensated by the promotion of good small ones. Despite the power and inertia of normal professionalism, the past two decades have witnessed shifts in the values, procedures and even balance of power within and between professions and organizations engaged with development. Donor organizations now seek to support more small projects identified and implemented by NGOs. More attention is given to people, especially women and others who are disadvantaged. It is not so much that the numbers of sociologists and social anthropologists in host governments and aid agencies have increased: they are still very few indeed (astonishingly, ODA still has only two Social Development Advisers).[1] It is rather that new ways of thinking and new values have diffused and been adopted and internalized by many others in other disciplines and professions.

These changes embody parts of the new paradigm and the new professionalism of development which have been emerging (see Chapter 1; also Jamieson, 1987). Key elements in these are reversals of the normal – to put people before things, to decentralize, to enable and empower the poorer and weaker, to value and work on what matters to them, and to learn from clients rather than always to teach them.

The very nature of the new paradigm makes its examples inconspicuous and easy to overlook or undervalue. Decentralized small-scale activities are less visible than centralized infrastructure. Social development is harder to see or photograph than physical development. Evolutionary change is less noticed than revolutionary. The enhanced capability of a resource-poor farmer to experiment and adapt is not as evident as a new pump or tractor. Perhaps because of its poor visibility, the paradigm is already more prevalent than some observers realise.

With projects and other development initiatives, one of the clearest expressions of the new paradigm and professionalism is the learning process approach (Korten, 1980, 1984b). Of this, many recent examples could be given. One is the OXFAM-supported Yatenga Project in Burkina Faso which followed two failures – a multi-million dollar soil conservation fiasco, and a small-scale attempt to introduce agroforestry methods from Israel. In contrast with these, a highly successful water-harvesting approach was finally evolved mainly from indigenous technology in a way which met the priorities of the people (Reij *et al.*, 1987; Harrison, 1987). Another is the Karnataka Social Forestry Project, supported by ODA and the World Bank. This has evolved continuously, learning from mistakes and criticism, and moving towards bureaucratic reorientation and decentralised micro-level planning. Yet another is the ODA-supported Integrated Rural Development Programme in Zambia (Mellors, 1987) which began in a technical blueprint mode and evolved into decentralized institution building, with an approach and procedures designed to encourage and empower local authorities. These examples show that the learning process approach is not limited, as some suppose, to NGOs. To the contrary, some donor agencies have moved towards it, as has ODA with its procedure of Planning by Successive Approximation (PBSA), used in the Karnataka and Zambia projects.

The blueprint and learning process modes have different implications for the early project process. This can be seen by examining their contrasts as in Table 1.2 (on page 12).

The learning process approach changes the early stages of a project. Project identification is no longer a discrete activity; it is continuous. In the blueprint mode, identification is a black, or at best grey, box, preceding the main procedures where the searchlights shine. In the learning process mode, identification is not a one-shot event, but an adaptive sequence of finding out what best to do.

Although they are presented here as dichotomies, the blueprint and learning process approaches can be and have been combined in many ways (see e.g. Rondinelli, 1983) with titles such as 'planning by successive approximation', or the 'structured flexibility' approach. Quite often such combinations will be appropriate. But the pull of normal professionalism towards blueprinting is so strong that without sustained reversals, the learning process pole has too little weight. No apology is needed for stressing it here. For better development actions, it should usually be much more to the fore.

Practical implications

To implement the learning process approach on any scale has many requirements and implications. Three stand out:

Calibre, commitment and continuity of field staff
The top priority is to enhance the calibre, commitment and continuity of field staff, and increase their numbers. They may be nationals or foreigners, and in Government or in NGOs, but unless they are of high calibre, committed, and able to stay for a matter of years in the same place, they are unlikely to nurture effective learning processes, involving as these do enabling, empowering, and institutional development. To quote a recent study:

> Two things are quite clear: there can be no successful development scheme without an efficient institution to push it through, and behind every efficient institution we will almost invariably find – at least in its early stages – an individual who is both an entrepreneur and an innovator. (Lecomte, 1986:116)

The learning process is staff-intensive, and requires good staff.

Restraint in funding
Too much money, or money too soon, or budgets which have to be spent by given dates, drive field staff into blueprinting. The budget which has to be spent in two weeks before the end of the financial year has to be converted into things, for example cement, which points to physical construction not human process. Large budgets mean buildings and machinery rather than self-help and self-reliance. Large sums thrust on NGOs tempt them to induce participation and to achieve early results through subsidies. These then prevent learning from participants, because poor people will undertake work in which they are not interested if they are paid or fed for it. Big budgets hinder learning.

Rapid appraisal
Continuous monitoring, learning, adapting, and appraising require their own timely and cost-effective methods. Rapid rural appraisal (RRA) now has a repertoire of techniques which makes it versatile, both for individuals and for teams. The International Conference on Rapid Rural Appraisal held at Khon Kaen University in September 1985 (Khon Kaen University, 1987) concluded, moreover, that RRA was not a second best, but to the contrary was often, when well conducted, superior to other known approaches. Its further development and widespread adoption are impeded by conservative normal professionalism, but it has shown its effectiveness in project identification (see e.g. Harvey and Potten, 1987). Its application for enabling rural people to analyse their condition and identify their own projects and priorities deserves further development.

RRA has a crucial part to play in the early project process. Given the early political irreversibility of commitment to many medium and large projects, rapid assessments in the very early stages can matter more than later longer studies and surveys. Such RRAs can steer projects before they are set in direction and form. They can also provide early warnings and help prevent bad projects. It reflects on the normal professionalism of aid agencies that they have not applied RRA methods more systematically in

85

the early project process, and have left their development more to universities and NGOs.

Learning projects

Dissatisfaction with the dominance of the project approach to development has provoked a search for complements or alternatives. A working group at Cornell University has christened a disparate family of these as 'paraprojects' (Uphoff, 1988). The family consists of:

- local capacity-building mini-projects;
- removing deterrents or lack of incentive;
- appropriate technology-cum-organization;
- planning and management improvement;
- savings-and-credit systems;
- horizontal diffusion;
- campaigns;
- bureaucratic reorientation;
- research and action programmes.

Uphoff identifies three general features of these: although funds are in most cases an important outside contribution, they are generally more labour-intensive than capital-intensive; they mobilize local resources including ideas and management skills; and their goals are qualitative change with quantum shifts in activity and outcome. The list serves to underline the range of alternatives to normal projects. Not all paraprojects, as listed here by type, are necessarily incompatible with a normal project approach; but they do show the importance of ideas, institutions, and the learning process: for initially at least, most of them would be difficult to blueprint.

Crosscutting some of these types of paraproject is an approach which follows from the key factors of calibre, commitment and continuity of field staff, restraint in funding, and adaptive rapid appraisal. This can be described as the learning project. In an ideal type of learning project, funds are available but no fixed capital budget has to be spent, and there is no pressure on staff to spend or to spend more; there are no targets for physical achievements; there is no preference for visible as against invisible change.

The essence of the learning project is good staff put in the field and sustained for periods of months or, more likely, years, exploring and learning from and with local people and trying to see how better they can gain what they want and need. With a learning project, it can take many months, even years, before substantial money should be spent, if it should be spent at all. Michael Shulz of Euro Action Accord spent 20 months in Port Sudan before making the first loan of a credit programme, a delay which caused consternation in headquarters: yet the programme was later hailed as an outstanding success. But the word 'yet' still reflects the old mindset. The success was not in spite of, but because of, the long gestation, the long identification, during which understanding and mutual confidence built up. Without the long, slow, exploratory start, it is unlikely that the second 20

86

months would have seen, as they did, no less than 1,500 small loan projects designed. Perhaps one of the great lessons in rural development is that 'identification', in its hurried and obscure normal professional form, is much of the problem, and patient and continuous learning and evaluation in the field are much of the solution. In this perspective, the learning project is not so much an alternative to the normal project as a different way of starting and continuing.

For the future, three needs stand out. The first is to see where a learning project approach has the highest pay offs. It may be with the diverse and complex farming systems of the resource-poor farming areas of the world, which are now such a priority for agricultural research. In these, new farming systems can require multiple innovation both simultaneously and over time, as was the case at Yatenga. Examples of such innovations are water harvesting and agroforestry. The second need is to develop institutions which can support learning projects with the necessary patience and flexibility. This entails changing rules and expectations. While NGOs have some advantage here, there is no reason why Governments and aid agencies should not do likewise. They will need, however, to protect learning project staff from pressures to spend funds. One device to this end is to draw off the pressure to spend by supporting parallel normal projects to absorb the funds. The third need is to train, inspire, encourage and reward the new professionals who make good learning project staff. That is difficult, but not impossible. Identifying a learning project means finding staff who are new professionals, and then supporting them in their extended local-level work, accepting that this may or may not later lead to the identification of normal projects. A start can be made by finding those who are already on the ground. For new professionals do not have to be invented. They are already working in many places, and increasingly support each other.

Conclusion

There are further implications for governments, aid agencies, and NGOs. To reduce the pressure to disburse funds, other uses for aid budgets must be found: debt relief and foreign exchange support are obvious candidates. Some necessary big projects can also help. At the same time, more staff are demanded by the new approach. Too many politicians and managers hold the peculiar view, perhaps traceable to adolescent readings of Parkinson's Law, that it is always cost-effective to reduce staff, described pejoratively as 'administrative overheads'. But reducing staff usually makes those who remain spend more time in offices and with paper, keeping them further from their poorer clients, and preventing learning. Many NGOs now know better. Much good rural development from which the poorer gain is staff-intensive, and the intensity has to feed right back into the donor agency. SIDA is being forced to cut its staff while its budget is raised. This perversity will probably reduce aid effectiveness. One defensive, if schizoid, device, might be to divide donor agencies into two: a big spending division with normal projects, and a high budget to staff ratio; and a learning project division with a low budget to staff ratio. In any case, more, not fewer, donor agency staff are needed by the new approach both in their headquarters and in host countries where they can increasingly be host country nationals. And Southern governments and Southern NGOs also themselves need more continuity in their field staff.

Finally, a step for all concerned, of whatever profession, discipline or nationality, is to recognize and offset the imprint in their minds of normal professionalism and normal project identification. When people are put first, and the poorer rural people first of all, it is more they who do the identifying and who set the priorities. At this frontier of the early project process, the question is not just identification *for* whom, but identification *by* whom. Some big projects will always be worthwhile, but one lesson of experience in rural development is that many successes start small and slowly and evolve through participation and mutual learning, with and by committed new professionals. Structures, policies and procedures can and should be modified to release them from pressures to spend and to give them freedom to explore and learn. The challenge is also to find, train and support many more of them. For the key to improving the early project process is not just changes in management, needed though they are, but more pointedly, better people in the field.

7 Thinking about NGOs' Priorities – Additionality and Spread

This chapter explores ways of thinking about priorities for organizations engaged in development, especially development NGOs.

Additionality is a basic commonsense concept meaning making things better than they would have been. This is seen in terms of the priorities of poor people, including their ideas of well-being, and enabling them to gain the adequate, secure and sustainable livelihoods they want and need. Higher additionality can be sought through exploiting the comparative competence of organizations, and through seeking wider impacts.

For NGOs, some of the best wider impacts come from starting small, exploiting their comparative competence in self-critical learning, and then passing on that learning to others. This includes developing, spreading and improving new approaches and methods. Lessons can be learnt from the NGO experience in developing and spreading participatory rural appraisal (PRA). Some spread has been through direct experience and contact – shared field training and staff mobility. Other spread has been through communications and sharing ideas and experiences. Quality assurance has been sought by stressing self-critical awareness and self-improvement. Potential wider impacts from NGO activities are changing with changes in NGOs themselves, in Government bureaucracies, and in communications.

A continuing professional challenge to many NGOs is to assess their comparative competence, to focus more on wider impacts, and for some, to work more on innovation and the spread of approaches, methods and institutions.

The context

A positive trend of the 1980s, continuing into the 1990s, has been the growth in the number, scale, scope and self-criticism of Non-Government Organizations (NGOs) concerned with development in the South. In the South itself, there are estimated to be some ten to twenty thousand development NGOs; and in OECD countries, some four thousand (Edwards and Hulme, 1992:77). Many NGOs have grown in size. Those who work in development NGOs (henceforth referred to as NGOs) have become more professional, both in the specialization and formal qualifications of their staff, and in their groping towards a new NGO professionalism. National and international conferences have been convened for and about NGOs (e.g. Drabek, 1987; Edwards and Hulme, 1992). Workshops where NGO staff agonise and brainstorm have become more common, as perhaps has self-critical awareness in the development NGO sector as a whole. Earlier, 'doing good' was sometimes thought to be enough. Now, the better development NGOs and NGO staff question themselves about what they do and do not do, what they should and should not do, and how to do what they should do.

These questions have come to matter more as the scale, scope and influence of NGOs has grown. David Korten's (1990:117) identification of four generations of development-oriented NGOs helps in understanding this. The first generation was concerned with relief and welfare; the second with community development; the third with the development of sustainable systems; and the fourth with people's movements. Of course, the generations overlap and coexist: relief and welfare, and community development, remain major and vital activities; but with the progression has come a shift of emphasis – to enabling and empowering as well as doing, to the long-term as well as the short-term, to the national and global as well as the local. NGOs now come in many sorts and sizes. NGOs in the North differ from those in the South in resources, access, power, and staffing; and their different roles and mutual South-North relations have become major concerns (Elliott, 1987; Kajese, 1987; Fowler, 1991). NGO activities are now very diverse. Especially in some of the poorest countries, and in some of the remotest areas, NGOs perform many of the service roles elsewhere carried out by government. The range of NGO activities elsewhere includes not only relief, welfare and community development, but also advocacy and lobbying, development education, legal reform, training, national and international networking, many forms of dissemination, and alliance-building. These varied functions and concerns, some of them new, coupled with the new relative importance of NGOs, challenge them to analyse needs and opportunities with more rigour, and to get better at seeing what best to do. In the past, it was more acceptable for an NGO to work locally without worrying about wider impacts. But now such a narrow view of NGO roles and responsibilities is more than ever open to question.

For this analysis, five interlinked questions can be asked again and again for any one NGO, concerning

- *clients.* Who and where are the NGO's clients?
- *needs.* What do they define as their priorities and needs?
- *means.* How can they be enabled to meet them?
- *comparative competence.* What is the NGO good at, compared with other organizations?
- *additionality.* How can the NGO really make a difference for the better?

Additionality: making a difference for the better

The concept of additionality helps to think this through. Additionality means making a difference for the better. In assessing additionality, four aspects deserve more attention than they usually receive:

- values: what constitutes 'better'?
- causality: what is 'a difference'?
- comparative competence: who best does what?
- wider impacts: what impacts can there be beyond the local and immediate?

Values: well-being and livelihoods

NGOs are said to be, and believe themselves to be, value-driven. The first question, then, is to decide what their values are or should be. Much debate and many answers are possible.

As a basic value, perhaps most would agree that life and conditions should be sustainably better for those who are poor, weak, deprived and vulnerable, enabling them to control more of their lives and gain more of what they want and need. Who defines what is 'better', and what needs are, are deep questions. In this respect, the shift of consensus among development professionals towards giving more weight to the priorities of poor people themselves is a move in the right direction, but still has a long way to go.

Two dimensions can help to elaborate this basic value: well-being as poor people themselves see it; and sustainable livelihoods.

Well-being as people themselves see it differs from economists' crude indicators of per capita income (see *RRA Notes* 15, especially Mukherjee, 1992), and often from ideas of well-being assumed for poor people by outsiders. An example of such an assumption is the persistent belief of administrators and urban elites that it is in the best interests of pastoral nomads to be settled, regardless of their way of life and wishes. There is no substitute for continuous efforts by outsiders to learn from poor people what they want and need, and then giving those wishes weight.

In economic crisis this matters, if anything, even more. Economic growth and higher and more stable incomes help for many forms of improved welfare, and will remain a priority for the poorer countries, not least because without economic growth, it is difficult to improve physical conditions and services (infrastructure, education, health, input supplies, transport etc). But even in economic stagnation or decline, improvements in well-being as people define it themselves can be sought and may be achievable if outsiders' actions can be fitted more closely to people's priorities.

A suggestive illustration comes from research in India. N.S. Jodha (1988) asked farmers and villagers in two villages in Rajasthan for their own categories and criteria of changing economic status. He compared these from surveys of the villages he carried out in 1964–66 and almost twenty years later in 1982–4. They named 38 criteria. Jodha then took the 36 households whose per caput incomes at constant prices had declined by 5 per cent or more and who were therefore worse off in conventional economic terms. He found that on average those households were not worse off, but better off, according to 37 of the villagers' 38 criteria. (The single negative was consumption of milk – in the later period less milk was consumed in the village and more was sold outside.) Some of the improvements (see Table 7.1) were quality of housing, wearing shoes regularly, less dependence in the lean season, and not having to migrate for work.

This suggests that even with lower real incomes, poor people can at least sometimes be better off in their own terms. This is not an argument for indifference to economic development. It is, rather, an argument for efforts to enable people to identify and state their own priorities, and for helping them to achieve them. This applies whatever the conditions. A paternalistic approach is unlikely to get this right. If their own priorities are met, people may

91

Table 7.1: Indicators of well-being in two Rajasthan villages, of households whose per capita real income declined 5 per cent or more over two decades

	Percentage of the 36 households	
	1963–6	1982–4
Households with one or more members working as attached or semi-attached labour	37	7
Residing on patron's land or yard	31	0
Marketing farm produce only through patrons	86	23
With members seasonally out-migrating for job	34	11
Selling over 80 per cent of their marketed produce during the post-harvest period	100	46
Making cash purchases during slack-season festivals etc	6	51
With adults skipping third meal in the day during the summer (scarcity period)	86	20
Where women and children wear shoes regularly	0	86
With houses with only impermanent traditional structure	91	34
With separate provision of stay for humans and animals	6	52

Source: Jodha, 1988

feel and be better off even in an environment of low economic growth or decline. Conversely, if their own priorities and criteria are not fulfilled, people can feel and be worse off, even in conditions of economic growth and prosperity.

The many priorities and criteria of well-being of poor people vary from person to person, from place to place, and from time to time. Health is often, if not always, one. In addition, a common and almost universal priority expressed is an adequate, secure and decent livelihood (Chambers, 1986, 1987). Livelihood here can be defined to include a level of wealth and of stocks and flows of food and cash which provide for physical and social well-being. This includes security against sickness, against early death and against becoming poorer. A sustainable livelihood includes reserves which can be used to meet contingencies (of sickness, accidents, losses, sudden or major social needs, and so on). It includes, thus, secure command over assets as well as income, and good chances of survival. Again and again, when they are asked, poor people give replies which fit these points. A phrase to summarize all this is sustainable livelihood security.

Causes and effects: the counterfactual and balance sheets
If well-being and sustainable livelihood provide goals and yardsticks, additionality in making a difference to them depends on the links between actions and effects. This presents two puzzles which, though commonsense, are habitually neglected: the counterfactual – what would have happened without the action; and the balance between good and bad effects.

Neglect of the counterfactual leads to misleading evaluation. An action can receive a positive evaluation because things are better after it, when without the action, things would have been even better; so the evaluation should have been negative. Or, an action can receive a negative evaluation because things are worse after it, when without the action, things would have been even worse; so the evaluation should have been positive. Whether things are better or worse is often influenced by changes in other social and economic conditions. One consequence is that where economic conditions improve, as say in Thailand in the 1980s, evaluations of actions are liable to be too positive, while where conditions deteriorate, as in much of SSA in the 1980s, evaluations of actions are liable to be too negative.

The assessment of additionality also requires a notional balance sheet. Bad effects have to be weighed and entered. With many development actions there are losers. Often these are the poorest, least visible people, and sometimes they are removed from the scene by death, migration or resettlement. Also, negative effects, especially on the poor, even when assessed, are often undervalued. Additionality is only positive if, on balance, the good effects outweigh the full negative value of the bad.

Comparative competence
At the level of an individual NGO, comparative competence points to what the NGO can do well compared with what others can do well. This is not static. NGOs change in their capabilities, through training, experience, recruitment, new priorities and procedures, and so on; and other NGOs and also Government organizations also change. But at any one time, an assessment can be made of an NGO's capabilities in coverage of geographical area and of types of activity, compared with those of other non-governmental and governmental organizations, to see where its relative strengths lie.

In practice, there is quite often competition between NGOs, or between NGOs and other organizations. This can have positive effects through healthy rivalry and improved performance. Competition can also have bad effects, where organizations compete to do the same things in the same places. If one organization duplicates another, or excludes it from an area or activity, then additionality may be low or negative. It depends partly on what the excluded organizations do instead. If some organizations do the easier and more attractive things in the more accessible and safer areas, greater additionality can be sought by others by working on harder and less attractive things, in less accessible and less secure areas, even if their performance by conventional criteria is worse.

At the level of civil society, there has been much discussion of the comparative competence of NGOs as a family of organizations. For many NGOs it lies in their relative smallness and flexibility, their staff commitment, and their ability to learn and adapt. This can be on the lines of David Korten's (1980 and 1984b) learning-process approach to development, contrasted with the blueprint approach (Table 1.2). The blueprint approach stresses preliminary technical surveys, top-down planning, and implementation according to time-bound schedules and targets. This is logical, often

93

large-scale, and except with infrastructure projects, rarely works well. In contrast, the learning-process approach starts small, hands-on, bottom-up, with action and learning before multiplication. The blueprint approach creates dependency, while the learning-process approach is empowering. The blueprint approach buries error whereas the learning process embraces it. Standardized blueprints fit well with hierarchical Government bureaucracy, whereas diverse adaptive processes are potentially and often actually part of the comparative competence of NGOs.

One key aspect is the ability to innovate and learn directly at the field level through action, learning by doing. Interestingly, this resonates with the advice of Peters and Waterman's book *In Search of Excellence* (1982), about America's best-run companies, where a chapter entitled 'a bias for action', starts with a Cadbury's Executive's injunction 'Ready, Fire, Aim' (Peters and Waterman, 1982:119). The message is not blindly to shoot off at anything; it is rather to start with action, on a small scale, to innovate on the run, and sensitively and quickly to learn from experience. Through such field-based learning, some NGOs have a comparative competence which, I shall argue, gives them an opportunity for additionality through wider impacts.

Wider impacts
Field NGO activities have effects and impacts which are direct and local, and indirect and dispersed. The direct effects and impacts have a natural primacy and tend to be more highly valued. They are more often explicitly stated as objectives, more physical, more measurable, and more limited to the defined and manageable geographical limits of a project area. It is direct effects and impacts that tend to be investigated and assessed by evaluation teams. Often, though, there are indirect and dispersed impacts that matter more. Typically, these are almost inadvertent, not stated as objectives, and less physical, less measurable, and less geographically bounded. Indeed, most of an NGO's additionality may lie in such wider impacts which pass largely unrecognised.

Many terms are used for wider impacts. The nearest synonym is externalities. Others include spread effects, ripple effects, and demonstration effects. Two of the most common words used in this context are replication and scaling up. Replication implies reproduction of more of the same. Scaling up carries overtones of an expansion of scale of operation, and has also been used more broadly. It is with such broader scaling-up impacts that Mike Edwards and David Hulme are concerned in their introduction to *Making a Difference* (1992). They distinguish approaches which are *additive* – implying an increase in the size of an organization and programme, *multiplicative* – where impact is achieved through deliberate influence, training and networking among organizations, and *diffusive* – where spread is informal and spontaneous. They further distinguish four strategies for scaling up or having a wider impact: working with Government; operational expansion; lobbying and advocacy; and supporting community level initiatives – catalysis, mobilization, networking and federation.

The term 'wider impacts', like the economists' 'externalities', has the advantage of being broadly inclusive. I shall use it to refer mainly to NGOs which support projects 'on the ground' or 'in the field'. I shall argue that they have opportunities for wider impacts which tend to be overlooked, undervalued and underexploited. For the purposes of the argument of this chapter, it makes sense to separate out and examine three of the strategies and types of wider impact: expansion, policy, and spread effects, the first two for brief mention, and the last for exploration.

For most field-based NGOs, *expansion* is the most obvious means to having more impact. It helps here to think in terms of David Korten's three stages: learning to be effective (learning to achieve what is sought); learning to be efficient (learning to be cost-effective); and learning to expand (Korten, 1984b). For some NGO workers, deeply engaged in the field, this is the obvious major strategy. Some NGOs, such as BRAC (the Bangladesh Rural Advancement Committee), the Grameen Bank, and PROSHIKA, all in Bangladesh, and SEWA (the Self-Employed Women's Association) and MYRADA in India, have extended their activities to an impressive scale. Such NGOs expand in different ways – laterally through replication in new geographical areas, vertically into additional activities, and diversely by encouraging different activities in different places.

Influencing *policy* is a second strategy, explicitly followed by some NGOs. Policy here refers especially to governments and donor agencies. Some NGOs which are centrally placed, like the African Centre for Technology Studies (ACTS) in Nairobi and the Centre for Science and Environment in New Delhi, have been very influential. Others derive strength from being field-based. Through their understanding of poorer people, their own learning, and their involvement at local and central levels with government and political leaders, NGO staff can gain insights and can influence government policy and practice. Lobbying, activism, and advocacy which are rooted in field experience carry weight. There are roles here of representative, communicator, interpreter and broker between local people and governments, or between governments and bilateral and multilateral agency staff. NGOs have a role of knowing and telling the truth about what happens at the grassroots. They can and do draw attention to the plight of the poorer and remoter people. Through NGOs' understanding of local effects on the poor of central policies – of structural adjustment programmes, of agricultural pricing, of forestry regulations, of anti-poverty programmes, and so on – governments and donors can be kept closer to the reality, and their policies made more humane. Arguably, NGOs' impact on government policies and practice is often greater than their more direct and local impact, and could be even greater if senior NGO staff gave it more priority. But policy influence is not easily measured or counted, and is sometimes diplomatically discrete, unseen, and unsuitable for annual reports.

Some of the widest and best impacts come in a third manner, through *spread effects* from field activities.

Of these the most obvious is the development, testing and spread of new technology, whether biological, software or hardware. Some NGOs with agricultural competence can, more easily than most government agencies, introduce new seeds, field and horticultural crops, multipurpose trees, livestock, approaches to soil and water conservation, and so on, and support

95

farmers in their experiments. If these agricultural technologies then spread on their own, as stable seeds can do, the benefits can be high indeed, and the subsequent costs to Government or to the NGO negligible or nil.

Another spread effect comes from staff mobility. Some NGOs, more than others, socialize their staff to become disseminators and self-starters – people who will go off and work in and influence other organizations, or start their own. For the parent NGO this may look like failure as staff leave. But the benefits to other organizations count as wider impacts, and the receiving organizations or new NGOs may then in turn become socializers of others. NGO A and NGO B might be similar in size and activities, but A might develop and send out staff who acted in these ways, while B retained its staff. A might do less well in the field than B, but its true additionality through the wider impacts of its diaspora of staff could be much greater. This points priority to staff development, to personal changes in people who work in NGOs, and to personal mobility.

Less consciously sought are spread effects through developing and sharing approaches and methods for development actions.

A few cases are well known where NGOs have made major impacts internationally through the dissemination and spread of new approaches and methods. Village community health workers were first evolved by NGOs, and then later adopted by governments. The Grameen Bank in Bangladesh has evolved an approach which has influenced the provision of small-scale credit around the world. Approaches to small-farm agricultural development evolved by World Neighbours have been spread through Roland Bunch's *Two Ears of Corn* (1985) and through other World Neighbours publications. The experience and methods of OXFAM have been shared in the OXFAM *Field Director's Handbook* (Pratt and Boyden, 1985).

Developing and sharing such approaches and methods can have a huge impact through adoption by other NGOs, but more so by government organizations. There are few examples like BRAC where an NGO operates on a scale which bears comparison with Government. In most countries, the scale and coverage of government operations compared with that of most NGOs is easy to underestimate. From a capital city, NGOs can appear to be doing a lot, but the observer is easily misled by being linked in with an archipelago of a few scattered islands of excellence in a country or region, overlooking the expanse of 'ocean' between them. It is the government, usually, which has the edge in covering that 'ocean'. If government adopts a good approach and methods, even if they are diluted and performance is spotty, the total wider impact can still be enormous, especially in large countries, simply because of the scale of operation.

Past examples, and the possible scale of impact, indicate the potential from methodological innovation. Generally, though, methodological innovation has been undervalued, and its dissemination relatively neglected. Nor are the generation and spread of approaches and methods always included in evaluations of organizations or programmes. This aspect of NGO impact, both actual and potential, is parallel and similar to the neglect of procedures in government organizations identified in Chapter 2. To examine this further, two examples of methodological innovation and spread will be examined and contrasted: rapid rural appraisal (RRA); and participatory rural appraisal (PRA), leading to the question whether, for NGOs, other similar potentials lie latent, waiting to be exploited.

The evolution of RRA and PRA

Rapid rural appraisal (RRA) emerged in the late 1970s as approaches and methods of enquiry about rural life and conditions which tried to offset the anti-poverty biases of rural development tourism (the brief rural visit by the urban-based professional) and to avoid the many defects of large questionnaire surveys (for which see e.g. Moris, 1970; Campbell, Shrestha and Stone, 1979 ; Gill, 1992, 1993). RRA stressed and continues to stress cost-effective trade-offs between quantity, accuracy, relevance and timeliness of information (Carruthers and Chambers, 1981). Methods and concerns include semi-structured interviewing, and the management of team interactions. In the 1980s, agro-ecosystem analysis (Gypmantasiri *et al.*, 1980; Conway, 1985a and b, 1986) contributed another powerful stream of methods including sketch mapping, transects, and diagramming. RRA came of age and acquired respectability not least through the international conference held at the pioneering University of Khon Kaen in Thailand in 1985 and the evidence, methods and theory presented there (KKU, 1987). RRA was seen as a flexible and cost-effective approach for outsiders to learn, with a varied repertoire of methods.

Participatory rural appraisal (PRA) is a continuing outgrowth from RRA. In the latter 1980s, and in parallel, the word 'participatory' was applied to RRA both in India through the work of the Aga Khan Rural Support Programme with the International Institute for Environment and Development, London (McCracken, 1988), and in Kenya through the work of the Kenya Government's National Environment Secretariat with Clark University, USA (PID and NES, 1989). Quite quickly, the term Participatory Rural Appraisal was adopted and spread, especially in South Asia (Mascarenhas *et al.*, 1991). Whereas RRA is extractive, with outsiders appropriating and processing the information, PRA is participatory, with ownership and analysis more by rural people themselves. With PRA it is less outsiders, and more local people themselves, who map, model, diagram, rank, score, observe, interview, analyse and plan. Experiences with PRA in South Asia, East and West Africa and elsewhere, have shown that local people are better at these activities than expected. We have witnessed a discovery of capabilities which earlier were little expressed and little suspected by outsider professionals, and often not known by rural people themselves.

From the standpoint of innovation and spread the comparison of RRA and PRA is instructive. The home institutions of those who developed RRA were mostly universities. The home institutions of those who have so far been developing PRA have been mostly NGOs. Other contrasts are summarized in Table 7.2.

The contrast reflects the comparative competence of some NGO staff in their work, access, attitudes and continuity. University staff have difficulty finding time to work in a participatory mode in the field, and for their purposes need to extract information quickly. RRA has offered them more cost-effective means of gathering data to process and write up. Many NGO staff, in contrast, live and work in the field, and increasingly seek not to extract information as much as to initiate, facilitate and empower.

The key innovations of RRA were methods. Methods were developed, adopted and described in agro-ecosystem analysis and RRA, such as semi-structured interviewing, methods for team interactions, transects, sketch mapping, and flow, decision-tree and causal diagramming, all carried out by outsiders. The creativity in devising and using these methods was that of outsiders.

Table 7.2:   RRA and PRA compared

	RRA	PRA
Period of major development	late 1970s, 1980s	late 1980s, 1990s
Major innovators based in	Universities	NGOs
Main users	Aid agencies Universities	NGOs Government field organizations
Key resource earlier overlooked	Local people's knowledge	Local people's capabilities
Main innovation	Methods	Behaviour
Dominant mode	Extractive	Participatory
Ideal objectives	Learning by outsiders	Empowerment of local people
Longer-term outcomes	Plans, projects, publications	Sustainable local action and institutions

The key innovations of PRA have been behavioural. Outsiders' ignorance for so long of rural people's capabilities has to be explained. The strongest working explanation is that outsiders (whether in universities, Government departments, research or training institutes, or NGOs) have believed their professional knowledge to be superior, and so have behaved in ways which have almost universally inhibited the expression of local people's capabilities. In the field, most outsiders find it difficult to keep quiet, to avoid interrupting people, to abstain from criticism, to refrain from putting forward their own ideas. Anil Shah, of the Aga Khan Rural Support Programme (India) has invented 'shoulder tapping' (Shah, 1991) to correct this – a contract among outsiders that they will tap the shoulder of any colleague who criticizes, asks a leading question, or puts forward his or her own ideas. The experience has been that for local people confidently and capably to express their own knowledge, to conduct their own analysis, and to assert their own priorities, outsiders have to step off their pedestals, sit down, 'hand over the stick', and listen and learn, which conflicts with much normal professional conditioning and self-esteem. The creativity in PRA is largely that of local people, and much of the innovation has come from them.

The comparative competence of NGOs here has been as facilitators, enabling and allowing diverse creativity. Normal university professionals and government bureaucrats seek standard approaches and methods. NGO staff have found it easier to tolerate and foster methodological pluralism. The questions raised for NGOs from the PRA experience are whether there are many other latent opportunities, through changed behaviour and attitudes, and through participation, for innovations to fit local conditions; and whether some of these will prove to have much more than local application, and so, much wider impact.

Modes of spread

In their spread, RRA and PRA have had common features. Both began as heresies. Both rejected conventional professional norms and behaviour, and developed and shared new methods. Both have been espoused and developed by independent-minded people. Both have faced opposition from professional establishments. Their modes of spread have spanned a common range, but also with contrasts, variously through training, through key people, and through sharing and self-spreading.

Spread through training
Styles of training have differed. RRA has tended to be taught didactically while PRA in its South Asian form has tended to be learnt experientially. To polarize the characteristics as follows is to verge on caricature, but helps to point up typical contrasts:

Table 7.3: RRA and PRA: contrasts in training

	Didactic	Experiential
	(more RRA)	(more PRA)
Aim	Learn methods	Change behaviour and attitudes
Duration	Longer (weeks)	Shorter (days)
Style	Classroom then practice	Practice, then reflection
Source of learning	Manuals, lectures	Trials, experiences
Location	More in the classroom	More in the field
Learning experience	Intermittent Intellectual	Continuous Experiential
Good performance seen to be through	Stepwise and correct application of rules	Flexible choice, adaptation and improvisation of methods

99

The more didactic mode has been represented by formal training. This sort of training typically takes weeks, starting with days of classroom preparation, with attention to the correct learning and performance of methods and sequences before going to the field. The six weeks of one RRA training course in Thailand was considered too short (Grandstaff *et al.*, 1990).

The more experiential mode of PRA training has been prevalent in South Asia and also elsewhere. Training has often stressed behaviour and attitudes more than methods. It has tended to take between 3 and 5 days, with 10 days as about the longest, often with outsiders camping in or near a village and interacting with villagers intensively from an early stage.

My own preference is for the shorter, experiential approach, learning by doing, making mistakes, embracing error, and improving. I have found didactic teaching inhibits, and leads participants to demand more and more time before they start in the field. In the experiential mode, one of the leading trainers in the Indian Government, Somesh Kumar, spent less than a day on briefing about PRA before sending people into the field for three days and nights, followed by a day's debriefing (Kumar, 1991). His emphasis was on behaviour and attitudes rather than methods. The short-term effectiveness of this approach was indicated by an experiment he carried out (personal communication). In one training, after initial orientation on behaviour and attitudes, one group was given only a sketchy idea of methods and sent straight out and told to get on with it; another group was first given a stricter briefing with do's and don't's for the methods before starting in the field. It was the first group, without the more detailed instruction on methods, that did better.

There are contrasting attitudes to manuals and their use in training. At their worst, manuals present closed codes of conduct which restrict, restrain and inhibit. At their best, they present an open menu of experiences, options and ideas which can be used selectively, or ignored. At different times and places, different forms of RRA and PRA have been recorded in manuals, guides and handbooks (e.g. McCracken, Pretty and Conway, 1988; Meals for Millions, 1988; NES, n.d.; PID and NES, 1989; Gueye and Freudenberger, 1990; Theis and Grady, 1991; Campbell and Gill, 1991). Their contents, style and uses have varied, from stepwise instructions for a predetermined sequence of actions, through compilations of ideas and experience from which the reader can select, to the manual of Krishi Gram Vikas Kendra in Bihar, with its single sentence on the first page: 'Use your own best judgement at all times' (Jayakaran, 1991), after which all other pages are blank (East African and Thai editions are believed to be in preparation).

Spread through key individuals
With RRA, and more so PRA, spread has taken place through key people who pick up ideas, hear about possibilities, have experiential training, or simply start, learn by doing and help others to learn. This applies especially to those who head small NGOs or departments in training institutes, and who have the scope to make changes.

100

A five-day PRA training conducted in Bihar in mid-1990 provides an illustration. Of some 20 participants, about 5 appeared to reject the approach, and about 10 were interested and enthusiastic, but were middle-level staff and probably not in a position to introduce it into their organizations. About 5 took it up, introduced it, and spread it. Three were heads of small organizations or departments: Ravi Jayakaran of Krishi Gram Vikas Kendra and Kamal Kar of Seva Bharati, both NGOs, immediately trained their staff and started PRA training for others in NGOs and Government; while Anup Sarkar of the Xavier Institute of Social Service, Ranchi, introduced PRA as the approach and methods for students' fieldwork. The short, intense experience had, thus, its main impact through a minority of participants who were well placed to take largely independent action.

The lesson is that spread of approaches and methods can be fast, efficient and sustained through key people who head small organizations which can then in turn train others.

Sharing and self-spreading
In the spread of RRA, formal publications have played a big part, especially the landmark volume of papers from the 1985 International Conference at the University of Khon Kaen (KKU, 1987). With PRA, the dissemination of ideas has tended to be freer and faster. Much has been through *RRA Notes*, sent without charge, a practically-oriented informal source of experience and ideas from the field. Spread has also occurred through small workshops, letters, telephone calls, sets of slides, notes on 'how-to-do-it', and word of mouth. With so much informal initiative, much of the process can be described as spontaneous or self-spreading. Two factors can be noted for their contribution to this process.

The first is practicality and pleasure. Unless done badly, both RRA and PRA are practical, and better for many purposes than available alternatives. Beyond this, PRA is usually enjoyed by both local people and outsiders, fascinating, and often fun. Practicality and pleasure combine to make PRA enabling and empowering as the process is taken over by villagers. The empirical finding, again and again, is that good PRA is both powerful and popular.

The second factor is sharing – of ideas, information, experience, and training. With PRA in South Asia, sharing was part of the culture from the start. MYRADA, a large NGO based in Bangalore but working in a dozen or more districts, adopted and developed PRA, and spread it among other NGOs and Government by inviting and welcoming people to its field training exercises. These often entailed camping in villages for several days and nights, a total experience which had its own impact on participants. Other NGOs in parallel and in collaboration did likewise, among them ActionAid, Bangalore; Activists for Social Alternatives, Trichi; the Aga Khan Rural Support Programme, Gujarat; Krishi Gram Vikas Kendra, Ranchi; Seva Bharati in West Bengal; SPEECH, Madurai; and Youth for Action, Hyderabad.

The degree of sharing could be exaggerated; but all of these have invited and welcomed others to their field training experiences in a manner which is not typical of NGOs.

Sharing has also applied to information. In contrast with formal journals, *RRA Notes* encourages photocopying. A deliberate attempt is made not to own ideas or methods but for them to be common property without attribution.

Spreading and self-improving

Much spread is degenerative: wider means worse. In this mode, as some RRA has spread, it has been done less well. The term 'rapid' has been used to justify rushing and sloppiness. Misleading findings have resulted. Johan Pottier's critique (1991) of hurried farmer interviews conducted in Northern Zambia warns of such error. Theo van Steijn's review (1991) of RRAs conducted by NGOs in the Philippines similarly points to quite widespread practices of low quality. In this mode, the label and the language of RRA have been used to legitimize bad work. The normal reflex to such degenerative spread is quality control from the centre, through manuals, setting standards, and training.

A contrasting mode of spread is self-improving. Some PRA as it has been spreading and evolving in South Asia, Vietnam, East and West Africa, and elsewhere can illustrate. To understand this, we have to see PRA as an approach and philosophy, a set of attitudes and behaviours. These include critical self-awareness, 'handing over the stick' (passing the initiative to villagers), 'they can do it' (having confidence that villagers can map, model, rank, score and so on), 'embracing error' (welcoming and sharing mistakes as opportunities for learning), and 'using your own best judgement at all times' (stressing personal responsibility). If these are part of the 'genes' of PRA as it spreads, then wherever it is adopted, practice should get better and better. Good performance comes then not from external quality control but from internal quality assurance, and through personal critical awareness, trying to do better.

This mode of spread might at first sight look like wishful evangelism. Missionaries who try to spread Buddhism, Christianity, Hinduism, Islam, or any other religion, are, after all, concerned with changing personal beliefs and behaviour. Basing analysis on the example of PRA, the self-improving mode of spread differs from the missionary mode in four respects:

Empiricism It is experiential, not metaphysical. It is based on what is found to work, not deduced from theory or drawn from theological dogma. Theory is induced from practice.

Diversity It is not concerned with uniformity. It invites and accepts rejection, and welcomes and embraces creativity and diversity of response.

Improvization It embraces uncertainty. We know that we do not know. We are dealing with conditions and processes which are unforeseeable. In such conditions, solutions which are reductionist, deductive, or preset rarely work well. Open-ended participatory improvization, drawing on a repertoire of methods, works better.

Responsibility   It places responsibility on the individual. In this respect, it resonates with some successful practice in American business management (see e.g. Peters, 1987:378). Even in some spiritual contexts, a paradigm of personal choice and responsibility may be emerging, as with the question 'If you were given the task of devising your own religion, what would it be like?' (Forsyth, 1991:264,277). In this paradigm, authority and responsibility reside neither in a bible or manual, nor in a sequence of ritual observances or procedures, but in personal judgement and choice.

Quality assurance is, then, sought through empiricism, diversity, improvization and responsibility, which hang together as paradigm, perhaps even as ideology. A forceful statement on these lines can be found in the last chapter, 'More diversity for more certainty', in *Development in Practice* (Porter *et al.*, 1991:197–213), analysing and describing a development project in Kenya. Self-improving strategies of spread fit this paradigm through their dynamic culture of adapting, improvizing, and creativity.

A growing potential?

The professional challenge to NGOs is to assess their comparative competence, and, for many of them, to ask whether there are new ways in which they can achieve wider impacts.

Paradoxically, thinking about wider impacts too hard and too soon can be a self-defeating diversion from doing well. The best wider impacts often come from starting small and modestly, learning, adapting and improving. If that is done well, some wider impacts come spontaneously or by linking in with government and NGO networks. But if wider impacts are sought, or even thought necessary, right at the outset for a new NGO, or a new initiative, then either size of operation through rapid expansion, or loss of learning and credibility through lack of attention to field realities, can distract. Much of the comparative competence of NGOs lies precisely there, in the ability, on a small scale, at the micro level, to question, puzzle, change and learn, and struggle to get things right. It is when things have been got right that there is much more to share; and getting things right may require concentrated and sensitive attention, especially at the start.

That said, the PRA experience illustrates how some of the comparative competence of NGOs can lie in methodological innovation, and then in the spread of new approaches and methods. It is a question whether there are many more potential new methods and approaches – in management, in research, in training, in behaviour, attitudes and interactions – waiting to be developed and spread.

The same applies with institutional innovation. NGOs have helped to develop many new institutional forms at the local level – women's self-help groups, groups of the landless, savings and credit groups, farmers' groups, community health workers, village volunteers and so on. Some have spread. Others perhaps could be developed more, and more deliberately disseminated as approaches.

Quite sharp questions are then posed. They include:

- should more NGOs pay attention to developing new institutions, approaches and methods, and then spreading them?
- should more NGOs make training one of their major functions, including training for Government staff?
- is there a role here for 'niche NGOs' (Cross, 1992) which are specialized, and which innovate methodologically and train for their specialization?
- should an ethos of sharing become more widespread in NGO work?
- should wider impacts be systematically analysed and included in evaluations of NGO activities?

On the basis of the PRA experience, the answers to all these questions look positive. Larger NGOs can ask whether they should redefine their activities to include more innovation, sharing and spread, and adopting and embedding in their culture and operations whatever good approaches and methods are being evolved elsewhere. Smaller NGOs can ask whether they should specialize and share. A model for a small, niche NGO is the International Institute for Environment and Development, the Sustainable Agriculture Programme of which has played such a prominent part in the international dissemination of PRA. Most such NGOs will, though, be field-based. In the right circumstances, a small NGO which gives priority to innovation, self-improvement, and dissemination, can have a huge wider impact.

This is not a static situation. There are other reasons for expecting that, short of some big human disaster, the scope and potential for developing and sharing new approaches and methods will grow in the 1990s.

First, the institutional cultures of NGOs are changing. Some NGOs still have closed vertical cultures – hierarchical, defensive, possessive, territorial and opaque. Such NGOs are less likely to share, spread, adopt and improve than those with open lateral cultures which are more democratic, undefended, and transparent. Except where fundamentalism is growing, the trend appears to be for NGO cultures to become less closed and bounded, and to move towards openness and sharing. Contemporary Christian NGOs of different persuasions, for example, show less competitive antagonism than their more missionary forerunners. Over the past few decades, the ideologies of development espoused by NGOs have quite often become more democratic, decentralized and tolerant. To the extent this is so, then self-spreading and self-improving strategies should do better in the future than in the past. Sparks spread fires where there is tinder; and there is more tinder.

Second, changes in government organizations though less marked, are quite widely in the same direction, especially where key individuals are committed to more openness, participation and flexibility. Other strategies for scaling up link in here. Government organizations are notoriously resistant to change, being typically hierarchical, given to top-down target-setting, quite often corrupt, and frequently misled about programme performance by false positive feedback (Chambers, 1992b). But there are scattered indications of reform, and reasons to expect it: increased collaboration at the field level between NGOs and government; more training of government staff by NGOs; more high-level recognition in democratic governments of a need to change; and in India, to be specific, requests from government organizations for training in PRA, and its use in the fieldwork of probationers of the Indian Administrative Service. In the 1990s more and more government organizations may well be open to adopting approaches and methods pioneered by NGOs.

The third factor is communication. To spread fires widely, sparks need not only tinder but wind. If NGOs generate the sparks of new approaches and methods, communications are a mounting wind which carries them. Communications are speeding up, penetrating, and persuading more and more. Despite contrary cases of local decline, disaster and dislocation, this penetration and linking is occurring in more and more places. It is a commonplace already to speak of the global village; and the 1990s are likely to see a world of human experience which shrinks and is shared yet more. The innumerable NGO networks and network letters, the floods of photocopies, the pervasive reach of radio, television and now video, and the spread of telephone, fax and E-mail – all these have augmented communication and sharing and can be expected to do so more and more. At the same time, many who work in NGOs are becoming better qualified and more professional, and more able and likely to use wider sources of information. Good ideas spread easily: participatory mapping (Mascarenhas and Kumar, 1991) has been adopted widely and fast, sometimes through seeing a few slides or pictures, sometimes simply through hearing about it. A good idea can now spread faster and better than before. Through informal communication, a new method tried in rural South India has been applied within a few weeks in Sierra Leone. Informal international networks are easier to create and use. *RRA Notes*, informally and quickly produced by the IIED, spreads innovations in a few months. Video is another powerful example: 'Participatory Research with Women Farmers' released by ICRISAT (1991) presents a new approach to agricultural research which in a matter of months was widely seen all over the world, both in its original and through copies which were made. Quicker and more effective communications have brought NGO innovators closer to each other and to other people and organizations than ever before.

All this means that the potential gains from developing and spreading new approaches and methods have increased and continue to increase. That strategy could and should then receive more attention. It requires innovation as normal practice, critical self-awareness as personal attitude, and sharing as institutional culture. The question now is how many of those in NGOs and government organizations have the vision, will and creativity to recognize this, and to give more priority in their work to developing new approaches and methods, and to their self-improving spread.

8 The State and Rural Development –
Ideologies and an Agenda for the 1990s

We have left undone those things which we ought to have done, And we have done those things which we ought not to have done, And there is no health in us.   *The Book of Common Prayer*

Successive ideological fashions in development have differed in detail but shared the same bias of originating in the cores and being imposed on the peripheries. In the 1970s, redistribution with growth was advocated through neo-Fabian extension of state organizations; in the 1980s, state organizations were to be slimmed in line with neo-liberal prescription. Neither ideology paid adequate attention to rural grass-roots realities, especially the conditions and priorities of rural people and of field staff.

Learning from the experiences of the 1970s and 1980s, an agenda for rural development in the 1990s can be based on an ideology of reversals which starts with the priorities and interests of poor rural people. The agenda varies according to local conditions, but has common features. Recommendations about the role of the state in this process are outlined, the guiding principle being that the state, besides protector and provider, should also be liberator and enabler for the poor, permitting and promoting for them both diversity and choice.

Ideologies and rural development

To generalize about the state and rural development in the South is rash. Almost any statement needs qualification. It is difficult to talk in the same breath about, say, Angola and the Andaman Islands, Togo and Thailand, India and Iran, or Cyprus and Kampuchea. Nations vary physically, economically and socially, and are politically diverse. Within national boundaries there are regional differences, and within regions ethnic, social and economic differences between households and people. Any commentator is also influenced and limited by personal experience, in my case largely in Sub-Saharan Africa and South Asia, on which this chapter is based.

These obvious problems have done little to inhibit the search for general policies and their dissemination. National policymakers need laws and programmes for whole countries. Aid agencies with large budgets, especially the Banks, need packages to promote. Academics need ideologies to dissect and denounce. Institutions and their members need and seek shared values and concepts to sustain solidarity and to support effective activities, especially where they have direct responsibility for policy.

106

And all these need a common language and set of concerns for dialogue and debate, for securing and legitimating flows of funds, and as a framework for thought and action.

Historically, the fashions for ideologies, packages, and programmes in rural development have changed. In part, this reflects changing rural conditions. The community development ethos and programmes of the 1950s, and the stress on agricultural extension and the dissemination of innovations of the 1960s, look dated and wrong now, even naive, with their stress on cultural obstacles to change, on community self-help construction, and on early adopters and laggards. Yet in the conditions of the time, they fitted better than they do now. The lesson is to see ideology and action in context, not as constants, but as arising from and adapting to, as well as moulding, those conditions. In this view, they are always likely to be out of date, always requiring an imaginative effort to be ahead of current convention. This could support a forced straining for originality, change for its own sake, and new fashions to sustain the market for consultants, advice, technical assistance, and research. What it should support is a continuous effort to see what best to do for the future. There will always be changing perceptions and policies. Given the centralization of power and communications with which we live, we have to generalize; not to do so is to generalize by default. The problem is how to do it better.

It is modestly in that spirit that this final chapter addresses the question of an agenda for state action in rural development in the 1990s. It approaches this with an historical view of neo-Fabian prescriptions of the 1970s and neo-liberal prescriptions of the 1980s, and then with a contemporary view for the 1990s, from below, of the rural conditions which both these have tended to miss.

Neo-Fabians in the 1970s: redistribution with growth
If the 1960s saw the zenith of national planning, the 1970s experienced only a slow decline. In a Fabian tradition, government organization was seen as a principal instrument for action against poverty. In many countries national plans had high profiles, and set styles and patterns to be followed also at lower levels, in rural regions and districts. In both decades, in sub-Saharan Africa (SSA), major and widespread attempts were made to prepare and implement district and even sub-district plans, with donor-supported integrated rural development projects following close behind. In South Asia, especially India, national programme followed national programme for rural development, to be administered through field bureaucracies. The pervading sense, supported by the best development wisdom of the time, was that government could and should do more.

A good illustration is the volume *Redistribution with Growth* (Chenery *et al.*, 1974), a joint study by the Development Research Center of the World Bank and the Institute of Development Studies at the University of Sussex. *Redistribution with Growth* (RWG) was inspired by the thinking and experience of ILO Missions, notably to Colombia (1970), Sri Lanka (1971) and Kenya (1972), and especially by Sri Lanka's outstanding achievements in health and education. It was also influenced by India's directly administered rural programmes. Significantly, Kenya, which received and influenced one of the ILO Missions, was closer to South Asian than to most African conditions in having a strong rural administration. Not surprisingly, direct administrative action by the state in rural development was taken for granted as a major mode of intervention. If not a bible of development in the 1970s, *RWG* was at least a revered text, cheap (my copy cost UK £1.40), accessible, and much prescribed and studied, as the heavily thumbed copies in the IDS library testify.

RWG is a prospectus composed by humane economists, having a second go after the planning fantasies of the 1960s. The authors had learnt the lesson that rural elites tend to capture the benefits of government programmes. They sought solutions through targeting: there were to be rural target groups, and urban target groups. In targeting the rural poor, asset distribution through land reform was stressed, together with services specially for small farmers, as in the statement that: 'A land reform which breaks the power of large farmers and the rural elite will . . . provide a framework within which public goods and services can be directed to the target groups with minimum leakage' (ibid.:135).

To provide these services, new organizations were suggested – 'wholly new institutions endowed with ample resources and the best cadres' (ibid.:68). An Agency for Small Farmers would conduct a co-ordinated programme with a package combining credit, crop extension, crop insurance, and input supplies (ibid.:128–90). The faith in direct government action, and the socialist sympathies of the time, are reflected in the opportunities seen in Tanzania:

> . . . we would stress that the lack of rigidity in much of tropical Africa makes possible interventionist policies designed to create new forms of rural institutions, such as the ujamaa villages in Tanzania, which can provide for the more efficient use of public infrastructure, agricultural capital, and such government-supplied services as extension, health care, and education (ibid.:135).

To reach and help the rural target groups, special institutions and programmes were needed. Economies, planning and the state were all seen in terms of growth. To do more for the poor, government must grow. The solution to rural poverty was not less government but more.

Neo-liberal in the 1980s: structural adjustment without a human face
If the 1970s were the decade of equity, the 1980s were the decade of efficiency. This is not to assert how much or how little either equity or efficiency were achieved, but to say that these were prominent in rhetoric and ideology. Efficiency has been linked in neo-liberal prescriptions with freeing markets and slimming government. In the 1980s, especially in SSA, but perhaps excepting Botswana, state organizations were seen as overgrown, inefficient, corrupt, and costly. The solutions advocated and introduced in structural adjustment packages included devaluation, which raises agricultural incomes from exports, higher domestic prices for agricultural produce, derestricting food grain movement, and deregulation of prices. Government recurrent

expenditure was cut back, and parastatals shrunk or disbanded. Even among those who opposed structural adjustment for its lack of concern for the poor – its lack of a human face – there was a degree of acceptance that governments should do less in some respects in order to do better in others.

A classic statement of neo-liberal prescriptions is *Accelerated Development in Sub-Saharan Africa: an Agenda for Action* (The Berg Report) (World Bank, 1981). This sought more efficient use of scarce resources. In his Foreword, the President of the World Bank said that administrative and managerial capacity were the scarcest resources in all countries. In that context, the report suggested that African governments should examine ways in which public sector organizations could be operated more efficiently and more reliance could be placed on the private sector. In agricultural and rural development, this implied competitive private input supply and marketing, and user charges and cost recovery for services. The solution to the problems of development was not more government but less.

Contrasts and commonalities
To polarize two schools of thought in this way is to simplify and even caricature; but it provides a basis for asking how they have been applied, what they have in common, and what they miss.

In rural development policy and its application, South Asia, especially India, contrasts with most of SSA in adhering to neo-Fabian approaches. It was, indeed, in India that some of the policies advocated in *RWG* originated, and where attempts to implement them have subsequently been most sustained. To my knowledge, India is alone among developing countries in its persistence with massive administered programmes targeted to individuals or households. These include the Small Farmers Development Agency (1971), Training Rural Youth for Self-Employment (1979), and the Integrated Rural Development Programme (1979), which latter continues into the 1990s on a vast scale all over the country. In a neo-Fabian mode, rural development programmes in India have been standardized, subsidized, packaged and targeted. That the packages often do not fit and often miss their targets, are commonplaces of field observation; but the approaches and programmes are stable. There are several reasons for this: some programmes are protected by misleading evaluation surveys (for a perceptive critique see Dreze, 1990); subsidized programmes play their part in local political patronage; the Indian Government, despite a rural population almost twice that of SSA, has had the financial and administrative means to persist with a rural development strategy in which field bureaucracies play a major part; the successes of the green revolution are seen by policy-makers as linked with the transfer of technology through agricultural extension and other services; and India has had the relative freedom from debt and aid dependence to be able to resist donor pressures to change its policies. In consequence, India's field bureaucracies show little sign of being eroded by neo-liberal thinking.

In contrast, many of the countries of SSA, with their declining economies, heavy debts, large government organizations, and weak administrations, have evoked and been subject to the neo-liberal prescriptions of structural adjustment. Both the state and the market have shrunk back. With recurrent budgets squeezed by smaller revenues and the conditions required by the IMF, World Bank and other donors, existing field bureaucracies have been starved of resources, with the familiar tragedies of agricultural extension staff without tyres for their bicycles, schools without textbooks, clinics without drugs, and teachers and health staff without pay. With economies in decline, basic goods have become scarce and costly. In places it has been NGOs, rather than the market, that have filled the vacuum left by the decline in government services. In India, the state tries to extend its activities to help the poor individually; in much of SSA, the state struggles simply to maintain some contact with them collectively and to sustain basic services.

These contrasts conceal commonalities. The Neo-Fabian and neo-liberal prescriptions of *RWG* and of the *Berg Report* respectively have in common that both have been elaborated and propagated by economists and in association with the World Bank. The authors of *RWG* were all economists – Chenery, Ahluwalia, Bell, Duloy and Jolly (though Bell and Jolly at least had rural field experience). Berg was also an economist. It may be no coincidence that while the *Berg Report* criticized the size of government in SSA, the one part to be strengthened was planning – 'The appropriate response now is to reinforce the central planning agencies, and to endow them as quickly as possible with the investment evaluation capacities they need' (World Bank, 1981:33). Both ideologies, and both sets of prescriptions, embody a planner's core, centre-outwards, top-down view of rural development. They start with economies, not people; with the macro not the micro; with the view from the office, not the view from the field. And in consequence their prescriptions tend to be uniform, standard and for universal application.

A counter-ideology of reversals
Centre-outwards, core-periphery views have their validity and strength; after all, since most power resides in the centre, it is in the centre that change can most readily be effected. But they also mislead unless complemented, qualified and offset by the reverse view, from the periphery. This amounts to a counter-ideology to those generated and diffused from the cores, whether Marxist, socialist, structuralist, or neo-liberal, and whether red, pink, blue, or any other hue but certain shades of green. It is a counter-ideology which takes as its starting point the conditions and priorities of rural people, especially the poorer, and the problems and opportunities which they face; and it leads to a different constellation of prescriptions.

The reversals have been elaborated elsewhere (Chambers, 1983, 1988). The switch or flip of view can be recognised by reflecting on the normal meanings attributed by professionals to the word 'remote', a word as profoundly as it is unconsciously urban-biased in elite usage; to a villager far from town it is the town that is remote. The reversals are of location, learning, explanation, values, control, authority and power, to put first the poor and the periphery.

When related to the role of the state in rural development, reversals provide an agenda for the 1990s. They point to two key aspects: first, the changing priorities of poorer rural people; and second, the conditions and behaviour of the government field staff with whom they interact.

For any urban-based outsider to state the priorities of poor rural people is yet another core-based act of paternal guesswork. But not to attempt this is also an act by default. Any statements have to be subject to qualification and change; and one of the greatest unmet needs in rural development is a continuous, sensitive exercise to understand the conditions, strategies and priorities of the poorer. When this is undertaken (as shown by e.g. Beck, 1989, Breman, 1985, Corbett, 1988, de Waal, 1989, Heyer, 1989, IDS, 1989, Jodha, 1988, Rahmato, 1987), the reality revealed can differ from beliefs commonly held by outsiders. Using these and other insights from field-work, my best inference is that many of the aspirations of poor rural people can be captured in the concept of secure and sustainable livelihoods, with access to basic goods and services, and freedom from fear and hassle. But priorities change, and differ; as the extended family and patron-client obligations have weakened, and as costs of services for health and education have risen, so command over assets to handle contingencies and buy services have become more important; and with rapid social and political change, and with more education and better communications, so self-respect has come to matter more.

For their part, field-level government staff have similar aspirations. They are often committed to their professional work but lack resources for it. They want and often badly need to earn more. Promotion is usually out of the question. Especially in SSA, their salaries have typically declined in real terms, eroded by inflation. Quite often, these no longer provide even for a basic livelihood. In Eastern Uganda in 1987 the monthly salary of a nursing aid would buy one kilo of sugar and two loaves of bread, and it required two months' salary of a secondary school headmaster to buy a bicycle tyre (Whyte, 1987:8–9).

Faced with the need and desire to increase their earnings, field-level staff who do not resign or manage to move to urban centres have two main strategies:

Moonlighting And Daylighting Clandestinely or openly, staff undertake economic activities. Farming and other self-employment are common. In part of Uganda in 1987 'agriculture was – for most professionals – the strategy of necessity which allowed them to remain professionals' (ibid.:12). In Burkina Faso it is known, and in Sudan it is widespread, for government field staff to be paid officially approved salary supplements by NGOs to work on the NGOs' programmes. Some activities are moonlighting – illicit and concealed; others, in countries as different as Sudan and Vietnam, are daylighting, carried out openly because they are condoned.

Extracting Rents The extraction of rents takes several forms:

(a) subsidies are shared. Subsidized programmes and inputs provide a surplus which can be creamed off. In India, for example, there are

111

standard understandings of percentages for sharing the subsidies for purchasing IRDP milch buffaloes.

(b) services are sold. Many practices are known. In much of West Africa, government rural health services have been *de facto* privatized. There and elsewhere, whatever small amounts of drugs are supplied are sold by staff, operating what are in effect private dispensaries. Teachers are paid by parents for admitting children. Officials are paid for moving files or providing documents. Irrigation staff are paid for providing water. Examples are legion.

(c) rents are extorted. Frequently, government rules give local-level staff powers which they can use to extract rents. Poor people are blackmailed with threats of persecution or prosecution. Payments are demanded for waiving restrictions. At the field level there are then conflicts of interest between poor people and poorly paid staff. Moreover, the less poor often pay less while the poorer pay more.

The perspectives of poor rural people, and the realities of field administration, are basic to the practical counter-ideology of reversals. This seeks to see things from the point of view of the poorer. In doing this, it is complementary to other ideologies, not an alternative. Macro analysis will always be needed as well as micro. But when generating agenda and assessing policies, core professionals normally neglect what poor people want and need, or assume they know what it is, or treat it as a residual. A balanced view can only be gained, offsetting and correcting core-based ideologies and views, by putting first the priorities of those who are poorer and peripheral.

In thinking through what the state should and should not do in the 1990s, three approaches help. The first is to learn lessons from the failures and successes of the past two decades. The second is a stance of eclectic pluralism, open to a mix of ideas. The third is this counter view, of reversals, starting with the perspectives of the poorer. The prescriptions which follow may fit neo-liberal tendencies in saying what the state should not do, and neo-Fabian tendencies in saying what it should do; but they do not depend on either philosophy. Based on reversals, they stand on their own.

What the state must do

(Everyone can read this section)

Three universal functions of the state are fundamental for the rural poor. It must do the following:

Maintain peace and the democratic rule of law
The appalling suffering and poverty resulting from civil disturbance and war is so obvious that it is easily underestimated. The fear, pain and anguish; the destruction, theft or loss of property; the insecurity of tenure; the disincentive to invest; the danger of loss of crops; the weak labour power when adults are fighting, guarding or killed; the interruptions to education;

112

the disruption of services; the distress migration and destitution of refugees – any listing of bad effects can start with these and continue with many more. The record of the 1970s and 1980s includes Afghanistan, Angola, Burundi, Chad, Eritrea, Ethiopia, Iran, Iraq, Kampuchea, Laos, Lebanon, Mozambique, Namibia, Palestine, Rhodesia (as it was), Sri Lanka, Sudan, Tibet, Tigray, Uganda, Vietnam, West Irian and Western Sahara, without even starting on Latin America.

The democratic rule of law is also fundamental. In some radical circles in the 1970s, democracy was seen as a form of Western cultural imperialism, and 'law and order' were dirty words associated with oppressive police action. Law can indeed favour the rich and the exploiters. Where force and intimidation prevail, as in much of Bihar, the poorest suffer. Where laws give power to petty officials, they may abuse it. It is the fairly administered rule of democratic law, and accessible justice for the poor, that matter.

Colin Leys once wrote on the primacy of politics (in Seers and Joy (eds), 1971). One can add the primacy of peace, and of fair laws and justice for the poor.

Provide basic infrastructure and services
Fiscal management of revenues and budgets is again fundamental. Beyond and based on that is the provision and maintenance of basic amenities to serve rural areas, such as trunk roads, railways, secondary and often primary schools, community and preventive health care, agricultural and veterinary extension, water supplies, weights and measures inspectorates, and in some areas telephones and electricity. Often, these are beyond the power of local communities to command and install or of the market to provide. NGOs, it is true, especially in some of the more afflicted states of SSA such as Sudan, have increasingly complemented and substituted for the state, and may do so even more in future. But the state remains the logical long-term institution to provide and maintain much of a country's basic infrastructure and services.

Manage the economy
Managing the economy, both externally and internally, is accepted by all except anarchists to be a legitimate and necessary function of the state, though views differ sharply on what and how much it should do. Three points relating to the rural poor can be noted.

First, the debate on pricing policy for agriculture (see Harvey, 1988) has not generated simple feasible policies applicable worldwide, given the conflicts of interest between poor rural producers and poor urban consumers; but higher prices for agricultural produce have often proved powerful means of enhancing the well-being of most poor rural people.

Second, parastatals for production support and marketing present a spectrum of monopoly and competition, and of performance. At one extreme is inefficient, overgrown and corrupt monopoly. Some West African marketing boards in the 1960s and 1970s are one example. Another example is the introduction of monopoly government organizations in some parts of India to market the minor forest products gathered by tribals. This

113

was designed to bypass contractors who paid little. In effect, though, it merely introduced another stage in marketing with its own costs, with the result that the tribals received even less than before (personal communication N.C. Saxena). In such conditions, it is common for field staff to gain power which they use to extract rents. Near the other end of the spectrum is the degree of democratic control and efficiency in marketing organizations achieved in Zimbabwe (Thomson, 1988). The question has to be asked, case by case, whether in the real, local world, poor rural people will be better or worse off with a parastatal marketing organization. Sometimes, but not always, the best solution may be plural, with a competitive private sector but a government agency providing a floor price.

Third, from the point of view of the rural poor, managing the economy entails much more than just ensuring growth, good prices and marketing: it also includes providing conditions with access to food and to basic goods at affordable prices, a function which some states in SSA have failed to fulfil.

An agenda for abstention

(Neo-liberals can read this section)

The neo-liberal critique of state intervention in the economy has included the size and inefficiency of government bureaucracy and of parastatals, with prescriptions that the state should do less and the market more. A full review of the scope for limiting or reducing state intervention to make things directly better or less bad for the poor would require a book of its own. Here, some illustrations must suffice, proceeding from the more to the less obvious and recognized.

Forced collective agriculture and villagization
Were it not for continuing attempts to maintain collective agriculture, as in North Korea and Ethiopia, this paragraph would be unnecessary. Only, it seems, with exceptional and voluntary ideological commitment, as with some of the kibbutzim in Israel, can producer co-operatives work at all well; and even the kibbutzim have had problems of sustainability. That Russia, China and Vietnam have been reversing collectivization is a recognition of the ultimate force of what most people want. That Russia is finding the reversal difficult is an indication of the powerful inertia of vested bureaucratic interests once institutions have been established. In SSA, producer co-operatives have been more important in ideological debates than in economic reality (Hedlund, 1988:12), and have performed badly; even *ujamaa*, the simple and limited form of collectivisation attempted in Nyerere's Tanzania, and remarked on positively in *RWG*, did not work.

Villagization induced by degrees of force has often been linked with collectivization, as in Ethiopia, North Korea and Tanzania, and as proposed for parts of Zimbabwe. The pros and cons have been the subject of much debate. The official motives are often a desire to control a disgruntled and dispersed peasantry. Against the officially-listed advantages of better access to services must be set higher health risks from population concentrations,

114

loss of control over and protection of land, including productive micro-environments, and loss of incentives to invest in more sustainable agriculture. Most important of all, villagization is rarely what people want.

It seems inherent in the contemporary human condition for most rural people to seek a secure and independent land-based livelihood where resources are controlled and commanded by the family and where returns are directly linked to efforts. With secure tenure and rights to land, livestock and trees, farm families tend to take the long view and invest in sustainable agriculture (Chambers, 1987). Without it, they take the short view and environmental degradation often follows. Not only are collectivization of agriculture and forced villagization undesirable as forms of core-based, top-down, ideological and political paternalism, which puts rural people's priorities last; they are also environmentally unsound.

Shining islands of salvation

Islands of salvation are small projects which receive special support and attention. Most governments deceive themselves and the international community through visits to these privileged entities, and through superficial reports and studies. Mick Moore (1991) cites the water co-operatives on canal irrigation in Gujarat, supposed by an international authority (Repetto, 1986) to buy water wholesale on a volumetric basis. However, almost all evidence of these co-operatives traces back to a single small project: the accessible, heavily subsidized, closely administered, and frequently visited Mohini Water Co-operative Society; and sustained searches by academic sleuths elsewhere in Gujarat have drawn an almost complete blank. The outcome is prescriptions which, as Moore shows, are physically and administratively infeasible, and worse, which distract attention from the main priorities for the poor. These are better management of canal main systems to improve supplies to the underprivileged at the tails. Or again, much of the insight and understanding about the progress and feasibility of *ujamaa* villages in Tanzania in the late 1960s was based on repeated visits to and articles about three special cases – the Ruvuma Development Association, Mbambara, and Upper Kitete. Generalising from these exceptional examples helped to mislead policymakers into a disastrous decade of trying to do what poor rural people did not want.

Borderline big projects

Not all big projects in rural development are bad. Few would wish to argue that the rural poor of Egypt would have been better off if the Aswan dam had not been built. Big infrastructure is sometimes needed, and indivisible. The case for heavy investments in communications and in power can be strong. There may also be a case for some large-scale flood control works, for example in the watersheds that flow into Bangladesh.

That said, the case against big new rural development projects has strengthened. Completing current projects, and maintenance and cost-covering for those completed, are often higher priorities than new construction. Complex projects have also tended to do badly. The World Bank's frank, sober and sobering evaluation of its experience with rural development from 1965–86 found an uneven record. Area development projects did worst, especially in SSA, leading to the comment that 'That form of area development project which came to be known as "integrated rural development" (that is, a multicompetent project involving two or more agencies) performed so poorly as to raise questions about the utility of that approach in many situations' (World Bank, 1988:xvi). While irrigation projects outside Africa did better, the position has changed now that many of the best sites have already been exploited. Those that remain tend to require the displacement of larger numbers of people, and they are often poor and politically impotent. The record with resettlement and compensation of oustees (though improving under pressures from the World Bank) is so bad that big projects are still likely to mean many poor losers. And when their livelihoods are given due weight in the calculus of gains and losses, appraisals are liable to be more negative.

Standard packages for diverse conditions
Normal bureaucracy centralizes, standardizes and simplifies. In capital cities, programmes are designed for whole countries and orders issued for implementation, regardless of diverse conditions. Targets, too, are set centrally and disaggregated to regions, districts and subdistricts, where they often make no sense. Agricultural extension, at its near-worst, promotes the same package of practices in different agro-climatic zones. Health services supply the same drugs to clinics regardless of local and seasonal incidence of diseases. Such standardization fails to serve the public, demoralizes staff, and has again and again been found wanting.

Controls which harm or exclude the poor
Many controls which make sense to central policymakers in practice harm the rural poor. The administrative reflex is to control and regulate for the common good; but with astonishing frequency, across a wide range of countries, conditions and domains, such control and regulation hurts the poor. Some examples can make the point:

Movement restrictions hinder work seeking. For refugees, restrictions on movement imposed by host countries can prevent migration essential for livelihood, and weaken their bargaining power when they do move, since employers can threaten to turn them over to the police. In consequence, their employment is less secure, their wages liable to be lower, and the danger greater of not being paid at all. More generally, freedom of movement for the landless and for poor rainfed farmers can be essential to permit migration to fill in seasonal gaps in work.

Effective nationwide price controls on scarce basic goods hurt the rural poor. Where the controls are effective, as in Zambia in 1980, it does not pay for rural traders to stock goods since they cannot cover transport costs and risks. Goods then stay in towns. Urban people have better access, and rural black markets, if supplied at all, have higher mark-ups (ILO/JASPA, 1981). Attempts by a central government to stamp out a black market, as with basic goods like paraffin, sugar, oil, rice and flour in Darfur in Sudan in 1984, only further push up the black market prices (Diab, 1988:44). The rural poor pay more or get nothing.

Restricted movement of food crops creates local seasonal shortages which the market cannot relieve. In Ethiopia in 1987, where such regulations prevailed, the price of sorghum at Degan market, on the main tarmac road from Addis Ababa to Assab, reportedly rose to three times its price at harvest, the highest prices being at just the time when poor people were having to eat less at fewer meals.

Regulations for minimum distances between tubewells in some parts of India protect the privileged access of those who sink tubes first. The restrictions do not deter the better off who have independent sources of credit: they can ignore the rules and go ahead anyway. The restrictions do exclude precisely the poorer who need institutional credit which requires that the regulations be observed. As so often, the haves have access denied to the have-nots (Tushaar Shah, personal communication).

Prohibitions on cutting trees on private land, and on their transport and sale deter planting, especially by poorer farmers who cannot handle contractors and the bureaucracy. In many countries, but on the largest scale in India, farmers are either prohibited from cutting trees on their land, or require permissions to do so. This means that even if farmers are able to cut, transport and market their trees, they get less for them. Of 12 cases reported by N.C. Saxena (Chambers, Saxena and Shah, 1989) of sales of trees or tree products in India, the highest receipt by the seller was 43 per cent of the disposal price, while in eight cases it was less than 20 per cent, among which three were less than 10 per cent. Cutting and transit restrictions were a major factor in price formation. Sellers were in a weak bargaining position, having to rely on the contractors who bought their trees to make the necessary side payments to the authorities. Though intended to conserve the environment to benefit all, restrictions on cutting, transport and sale discriminate against the poorer and weaker, induce them to cut and sell while they can, and discourage them from replanting. Poor people's private trees are savings, but in these conditions they can only cash them on bad terms. To restrict harvest, transit and sale is like a bank manager refusing withdrawals; not surprisingly this inhibits deposits – tree planting – especially by the poorer. There is probably no measure so easy, quick and vast in impact, and which would help poorer farmers and the environment more, than the abolition of such rules.

Restrictions such as these – on movement of people, on retail prices for scarce basic goods, on movements of food grains, on sinking tubes for groundwater, and on the harvest, transit and sale of private trees – are manifestations of the disabling state. Whatever their intentions, in practice such rules impoverish and deprive the rural poor – by loss of opportunities for earning; by denial of access to productive resources; by disincentives for saving; by less to buy and higher prices; and by the hassles, uncertainties

117

and costs of dealing with rent-seeking officials or those who can pay them off. Those who are less poor and more influential can flout or bypass regulations, while the poorer are excluded, or have to pay. Not always, but all too often, restricted access and imperfect markets penalize poor rural people. Again and again, they want the state off their backs. One of the quickest and easiest ways for the state to help poor rural people on a large scale is to abolish damaging restrictions, to dismantle the disabling state.

For neo-liberals who want the state to wither more than somewhat, these points may warm the heart. They should provide an acceptable and practical agenda. But let them not relax and rejoice too soon, for there is more to come.

An agenda for action

(Neo-Fabians can read this section)

Normal bureaucracy: doing the do-able
Since field bureaucracies normally centralize, standardize and simplify, it is commonsense to give them tasks for which these tendencies are strengths. These are of two types.

The first is where a standard receiving environment can be found or created, suitable for a standard input. Immunization for people or livestock is an example, with simple one-off inputs into the closely controlled and predictable environment of the human or animal body. To differing degrees the GOBI (growth charts, oral rehydration, breast feeding, and immunization) programmes promoted by UNICEF lend themselves to simple repetition, and have scored successes in child welfare even in bad economic conditions such as those in Zimbabwe in 1982–4 (Cornia *et al.*, 1987:290). Sometimes, too, uniform environments can be created, as when irrigation and fertilizer modify the farm environment to fit green revolution genotypes.

The second feasible task for normal field bureaucracies is the transfer or supply of technology which is robust and usable in a wide range of conditions. In India, the Technology Missions based in the Prime Minister's office at the time of Rajiv Gandhi stressed high quality blackboards and good handpumps. Blackboards and handpumps can be designed and made to work well almost anywhere, given schools and groundwater respectively. It is again the do-able that is being done.

Safety nets
Almost all poor people, including many of the ultra poor or near-destitute, struggle hard, even desperately, to avoid becoming even poorer; but they are vulnerable to contingencies. When bad years and disasters strike, they are further impoverished, whether through sale of assets, new debts, new obligations, or physical disability. Big health-care costs are one new threat to the poor who have a sick relative; they can impoverish utterly, reinforcing the case for effective free or cheap treatment. Once impoverished by loss of productive assets, say in a famine, recovery is hard. To help those who have become poorer to claw back to their previous condition is costly

and difficult, although there have been successes, as shown by experience with OXFAM-supported restocking programmes for pastoralists in Kenya (Moris, 1988). In general, though, it is likely to be much more cost effective, as well as more humane, to provide safety nets to help poor people avoid becoming poorer in the first place.

Measures to do this are many. They include: public works and food for work programmes, among which the Maharashtra Employment Guarantee Scheme provides a model in which groups of people can demand work paid at the minimum wage; early interventions to keep food prices down and incomes up at bad times, for example by buying at good prices whatever poor people decide to sell (livestock, jewellery, charcoal etc); when famine threatens, food or other relief provided early enough to prevent the poorer having to dispose of their assets, together with clean water and immunisation (de Waal, 1989); and at all times, effective preventive and curative health services available free or at low cost. Also, wherever the state has the resources and capacity, and social supports are feeble, there is a case for help for the destitute and indigent, as provided for widows in some Indian states.

The weaker the state, the greater the part NGOs can have to play; but in most countries, at most times, it is to the state that the safety-net role falls.

Changing rules
The micro perspective, from below, can reveal scope for gains by the poorer from changing rules. Tushaar Shah's fieldwork on groundwater markets in India, coupled with economic analysis, led to a switch of electricity charging policy in Gujarat, from pro rata to graduated per horse-power rates. This resulted in between 1.5 and 2 million buyers of irrigation water (generally the poorer and smaller farmers) paying 25 and 60 per cent less to sellers (Chambers, Saxena and Shah, 1989). The question is whether this was a unique opportunity, or whether other fieldwork and analysis could reveal other simple changes with similar vast, quick impact. At the very least, micro-level investigation merits attention to search for other potentials.

Secure rights and information
The poorer people are, the more they need secure rights. To enjoy their rights, they need to know what they are and how to claim them. They also often need organization and solidarity to overcome vested interests. Two aspects can illustrate the potential here.

First, where restrictions are abolished, the changes must be credibly known. In India a forester has told me that although in law no restrictions on movement of certain trees applied, the Forest Department pretended to the public that they did. A first step in the reversal of power needed in such a case is information, and then encouragement, through countervailing organization, and even through changes in the judicial system, for people to claim their rights, resist extortion, and eliminate hassle.

Second, for resource-based livelihoods to be sustainable, rights and access to the resources must be secure. Without secure tenurial rights, groups

119

and families lack the incentive for long-term investment in land, water, pasture, soils and trees. In practice, it is precisely the more fragile environments – forests, uplands, swamps, wetlands, semi-arid savannahs, and arid pastures – disparate though they are ecologically, where tenure is least secure and least exclusive. Urban-based interests sometimes seek to gain or maintain open access and to deny exclusive tenurial rights to communities or individuals; and this can reinforce the common failure in central places of policy-making to recognize the importance of secure tenure to those who seek their livelihoods in such remote and ecologically vulnerable areas.

Communication of their rights to poor and scattered rural people is perhaps the most promising frontier for the state in rural development in the 1990s. In contrast with earlier decades, it will be easier to inform peripheral people about changes in regulations and rights. The revolution in communications is already reaching the most remote places. Using multiple channels – radio, television, video, newspapers, handbills, noticeboards, meetings – public information and public consultations will be more credible and convincing. It will be harder to mislead the poor at the local level. The benign state cannot be assumed, and communications can be used for many bad purposes. Where, though, there is central desire to inform and empower through credible and correct information, the means to do so will more and more be there. Communications are a cornerstone of an enabling state.

Reversals, diversity and the enabling state

The prescriptive paradigm of reversals for rural development is neither neo-Fabian nor neo-liberal. Nor is it just eclectic pluralism. Putting poor rural people first provides starting points which are at once dispersed, diverse and complicating. Linear teleology in development thinking has long since fallen from favour (for critiques see e.g. Nettl, 1969 and Streeten, 1983:881–3) but linear measures of development along scales (per caput GNP, infant mortality rate, female literacy) persist as universal tools of assessment and comparison. They are needed, but they condition analysts to think in linear terms. In contrast, field-level realities – whether ecosystems, farming systems, or livelihood strategies – are non-linear, adaptive and differentiating. For some professionals, development is still, consciously or unconsciously, seen as convergent; in the paradigm of reversals, development is decentralised and divergent. While normal bureaucracy and normal markets centralise, standardize and simplify, it is in contrast by becoming more complex and diverse that ecosystems and livelihood strategies become more stable and more sustainable.

Near the core of this paradigm is decentralized process and choice. One expression of this is farmer participatory research for resource-poor agriculture (Farrington and Martin, 1988; Chambers, Pacey and Thrupp, 1989). This is coming to stress not the transfer of technology in the form of packages of practices for the uniform, simple, controlled environments of the irrigated green revolution, but provision of baskets of choices for the more diverse, complex and risk-prone farming systems of rainfed agriculture. Bureaucratic reversals are implied, with varied local requests passed up from farmers replacing pre-set technologies passed down to them. Approaches which put farmers' analysis and priorities first complement those which generate and transfer technology. In this mode, the state is not school but cafeteria, and development is decentralized, becoming not simpler but more complex, and not uniform but more diverse.

The paradigm of reversals takes us even further; for it resolves the contradiction between the neo-Fabian thesis that the state should do more, and the neo-liberal antithesis that the state should do less. In terms of this paradigm, the state has often done those things which it ought not to have done, and has left undone those things which it ought to have done. The patterns vary and diverge. In much of SSA the state has been so weakened that it has retracted too far, and made errors of omission. In India it has extended too far, and made errors of commission. The worst mistakes have been rules and restrictions which give field-level staff power to extract rents from the weak. Here a new neo-liberal agenda can liberate the poor by abolishing the regulations used to exploit them. The task is to dismantle the disabling state. In parallel, there is more that the state can and should do. Here a new neo-Fabian agenda can decentralize while providing safety nets, secure rights and access to reliable information, and permitting and promoting more independence and choice for the poor. The task is to establish the enabling state. For both these new agendas, the unifying theme is reversals, to put first the diverse priorities of poor people. To understand and support these is equitable – helping people gain what they want, efficient – mobilizing their creative energy, and sustainable – providing incentives for long-term self-reliant investments by the poor. The vision is then of a state which is not only protector and supporter, but also enabler and liberator; and of the 1990s as a decade for equity and efficiency through reversals and diversity.

Notes

CHAPTER 1

1. This view has been challenged. Wegener held a doctorate in astronomy and did indeed earn his living much of his life as a meteorologist. But Nield (1986) disputes the idea that his being a meteorologist was why his theory was scorned, this being 'the one thing even the daftest first-year student manages to remember about the history of the theory of continental drift.' Nield implies that Wegener's failure to protect his image was significant. He contrasts the damaging effects of Wegener's unconcealed eccentricity with Charles Dodgson's careful separation of his identity as a mathematician from that of the author of Alice in Wonderland.

CHAPTER 2

1. This expression is borrowed from Warren Ilchman. See also Ilchman and Uphoff, 1971: 260–2.

CHAPTER 3

1. Joseph Ssennyonga, personal communication.
2. This generalization is justified by the concentration in this chapter on 'top-down' projects, i.e. projects which involve government planning of implementation. Poverty-orientated rural projects may be very rapidly implemented where they originate in popular enthusiasm.
3. This reliable information was given on condition that in quoting it the source would not be given.
4. Myths are perpetuated because the evidence for statements of this sort is usually informal personal communication rather than the printed word. For obvious reasons, sources for the illustrations given here cannot be cited. But examples reported to the writer by experienced practitioners of cost-benefit analysis include the following. A multilateral agency wished to finance a livestock project. The appraisal team estimated a rate of return of 11 per cent, only to be sent a cable from the organization's headquarters telling them to make it 15. Or gain, an appraisal team, after months of work on an electricity project, visited a senior official and told him that the rate of return would be 9 per cent only to be told 'Come back tomorrow when it is 14'. Or again, a senior official responsible for preparing and submitting projects to donors always decided the rate of return first and then instructed his staff to produce it. It is not easy to assess how common such practices are; but it is extraordinary that the informal quality of decisionmaking is not more seriously treated in the manuals on project appraisal. An honourable exception is the OXFAM Handbook for its Field Directors (1976:5) which states, for example 'The danger of using shadow prices is that they may be over- or underestimated in order to justify projects to which the appraiser feels personally committed'.
5. Squire and van der Tak do, however, briefly consider the costs and benefits of their proposals. They believe that the benefits justify the costs, but note nevertheless that 'the initial cost of transition to the new methodology is substantial,

122

since users must become familiar with the new techniques, and initial estimates of country parameters for shadow-pricing must be built up' (1975:10).

6. When this proposal was put to a senior UN official, he was against it because of the health risks his officials would face from living in villages.

CHAPTER 4

1. Quoted in G.J. Gill *Seasonality and Agriculture in the Developing World: a problem of the poor and powerless*, Cambridge University Press 1991.
2. An earlier version of this chapter was published as 'Rural Health Planning: Why Seasons Matter', in Kerr L. White and Patricia Bullock (eds), *The Health of Populations*, The Rockefeller Foundation, Sept. 1980. I am grateful to over 50 people, too numerous to name, for criticism, comment and information.
3. See also Postscript to the chapter, page 57.
4. Warrell and Arnett consider that 'Although snake bite is recognized locally as an important medical problem in many rural areas of the tropics, its incidence has been grossly under-reported'. High incidence is associated with farming activities and with rains which drive snakes to drier land (pp.320 and 326).
5. The mean for mothers in families with two acres or more was 41.8 kg and for landless mothers 40.2 kg. Both groups weighed most in March and least in September, with percentages of their respective means of 103 and 104 for March, and 97 and 95 for September.
6. Personal communications, Saleha Begum, Martin Greeley, and members of the field team of the Institute of Development Studies Project on Post-Harvest Losses in Bangladesh.
7. For these and other biases against perceiving rural poverty, see Chambers (1981a and 1983: 10–23).
8. For discussion of learning from rural people, see IDS (1979).
9. For example, a manual for assessing rural needs warns about the unexpected in rural surveys and says: 'once, the jeeps needed for transporting the interviewers were recalled for a month *during the few precious months of the dry season*' (my emphasis), (Ashe, 1979: 26).
10. Consider, for example, the social and economic cost to a poor family of persuading the able-bodied at a time of peak activity to carry a sick person to a clinic for treatment, if indeed they could so persuade anyone.
11. See for example, Cole-King (1979: 8), 'Patients frequently have to wait long hours at out-patient facilities; if they have to travel any distance, and visit to a health centre may take a whole day, the loss of a day's work may be a significant cost to patients'.
12. If services are inelastic, those seeking treatment have to wait longer at peak periods, fewer of those who are sick will come for treatment, and those operating the services will underestimate morbidity in the population as a whole. Alastair White (personal communication) reports '. . . in El Salvador where treatment is rationed in a queuing basis (the doctor will be able to see say 30 patients in the day, so it is only the first 30 to arrive who are seen), high seasonal demand is translated into a need to arrive earlier, which will mean setting out from home before dawn if you live in a village a couple of miles away, even though the doctor does not arrive till 9 a.m.'
13. The 1978 Report of the Gono Unnayan Prochesta (People's Development Effort), Bangladesh (GUP, 1979), is illuminating. Patients at the Outdoor Clinic, Khalia, reached a peak of 9.830 in June, and dropped to 1.227 in December. The high figure in June was partly associated with high morbidity, but also with less work to do in the fields, ease of travel, and cash from paddy and jute

harvests; while December was a busy month with harvesting and post-harvest processing for the main paddy crop.

14. A question raised here is whether traditional medical practitioners receive a disproportion of patients during the rains, with a compensating seasonality in attendances between traditional (rains) and allopathic (dry season) services and practitioners. Any such tendency might be reinforced by financing arrangements, with debts easier to arrange in the traditional than in the allopathic system.

15. The work of Margaret Haswell (1975; 1981) in Genieri village and of the Dunn Nutrition Unit at Cambridge University (see Rowland *et al.*, 1981 for references) in Keneba village.

16. The work of Richard Longhurst (1979), David Norman, Emmy Simmons (1981), Andrew Tomkins (1981), Michael Watts (1981) and others based on Ahmadu Bello University, Zaria.

17. The work of the Cholera Research Laboratory, Dacca (see Chowdhury *et al.*, 1981 for references) in Matlab Thana, Comilla District.

18. This is partly an inference from Dasgupta's (1975) comparative analysis of 126 Indian villages.

19. For an elaboration of this sort of approach, see Chambers (1974).

CHAPTER 6
1. ODA has increased its social development advisers from 2 in 1988 to 11 in March 1993.

References

Abedin, Z. and Fazlul H., (1989) 'Innovator Workshops in Bangladesh', in Chambers, Pacey and Thrupp (eds) *Farmer First*, Intermediate Technology Publications, London, pp. 132–136.

Amanor, J., (1989) *340 Abstracts on Farmer Participatory Research, Agricultural Administration (Research and Extension) Network Paper* Number 5, ODI, London June.

Ashby, J., (1984) 'Participation of Small Farmers in Technology Assessment', International Fertiliser Development Center.

Ashby, J.A., (1990) *Evaluating Technology with Farmers: A handbook*, IPRA Projects, CIAT, December.

Ashby, J., Quiros, C. and Riviera, Y., (1987) 'Farmer participation in on-farm varietal trials', *Discussion Paper* 22, Agricultural Administration (Research and Extension) Network, Overseas Development Institute, London, December.

Ashe, J., (1979) *Assessing Rural Needs: a Manual for Practitioners*, Mt. Rainier, Maryland; VITA (Volunteers in Technical Assistance).

Bagadion, B.U. and Korten, F.F., (1985) 'Developing Irrigators' Organizations: A Learning Process Approach', in M. Cernea (ed.) *Putting People First*, OUP for the World Bank.

Baker, G., Knipscheer, H. and de Souza Nieto, J., (1988) 'The Impact of Regular Research Field Hearings (RRFH) in On-farm Trials in Northeast Brazil', *Experimental Agriculture*, 24, Part 3, pp. 281–288.

Barrell, R.A.E. and Rowland, M.G.M., (1979) 'Infant Foods as a Potential Source of Diarrhoeal Illness in Rural West Africa', *Transactions of the Royal Society of Tropical Medicine and Hygiene*, Vol. 73, No. 1, pp. 85–90.

Bayliss-Smith, T., (1981) 'Seasonality and Labour in the Rural Energy Balance', in Chambers, Longhurst and Pacey *Seasonal Dimensions to Rural Poverty*, Frances Pinter, London, pp. 30–38.

Beck, T., (1989) 'Survival strategies and power amongst the poorest in a West Bengal village', *IDS Bulletin* Vol. 20, No. 2, April.

Becker, S. and Sardar, M.A., (1981) 'Seasonal Patterns of Vital Events in Matlab Thana, Bangladesh', in Chambers, Longhurst and Pacey *Seasonal Dimensions to Rural Poverty*, Frances Pinter, London, pp. 149–154.

Belcher, D.W., Wurapa, F.K., William, B. and Lourie, I.M., (1975) 'Guinea Worm in Southern Ghana: Its Epidemiology and Impact on Agricultural Productivity', *American Journal of Tropical Medicine and Hygiene*, Vol. 24, No. 2, pp. 243–9.

Bentley, J.W. and Melara, W., (1991) 'Experimenting with Honduran Farmer-Experimenters', *Research Note* in *ODI Agricultural Administration (Research and Extension) Network Newsletter* 24. June, pp. 31–48.

Bergmann, H. and Boussard, J-M., (1976) *Guide to the Economic Evaluation of Irrigation Projects*, OECD, Paris.

Bhambore, S.R. *et al.* (1952) 'A survey of the economic status of villagers in a malarious irrigated tract in Mysore State, India, before and after DDT residual insecticidal spraying', *Indian Journal of Malariology*, Vol. 6, pp. 355–65.

Bos, M.G. and Nugteren, J., (1974) *On Irrigation Efficiencies*, International Institute for Land Reclamation and Improvement, Wageningen.

Bowman, W.E., (1956) *The Ascent of Rum Doodle*, MacDonald and Company.
Bray, R.S., (1991) 'Insect-borne Diseases: Malaria' in Chambers, Longhurst and Pacey *Seasonal Dimensions to Rural Poverty*, Frances Pinter, London, pp. 116–120.
Breman, J., (1985) *Of Peasants, Migrants and Paupers: Rural Labour Circulation and Capitalist Production in West India*, OUP, Delhi, Bombay, Calcutta and Madras.
Brokensha, D., Warren, D.M. and Werner, O. (eds) (1980) *Indigenous Knowledge Systems and Development*, University Press of America, Lanham MD20801.
Bunch, R., (1985) *Two Ears of Corn: a guide to people-centered agricultural improvement*, World Neighbors, Oklahoma.
— (1987) 'Case Study of Guinope Integrated Development Programme, Guinope, Honduras', paper for Only One Earth: Conference on Sustainable Development, organized by the International Institute for Environment and Development, London, 28–30 April.
— (1989) 'Encouraging Farmers' Experiments' in Chambers, Pacey and Thrupp (eds) *Farmer First*, Intermediate Technology, London, pp. 55–61.
Bunting, A.H., (1970) 'Review and Conclusions', in A.H. Bunting (ed.), *Change in Agriculture*, Duckworth, London, pp. 715–793.
Burns, T. and Stalker, G.M., (1961) *The Management of Innovation*, Tavistock Publications, London.
Butterfield, H., (1949), *The Origins of Modern Science*, Bell and Sons, London.
Byerlee, D., (1987) 'Maintaining the Momentum in Post-Green Revolution Agriculture: A Micro-level Perspective from Asia', *MSU International Development Paper* No 10, Department of Agricultural Economics, Michigan State University, East Lansing, Michigan 48824.
Caiden, N. and Wildavsky, A., (1974) *Planning and Budgeting in Poor Countries*, John Wiley and Sons, New York, London, Sydney and Toronto.
Campbell, J.G., Shrestha, R. and Stone, L., (1979) *Uses and Abuses of Social Science Research in Nepal*, Research Centre for Nepal and Asian Studies, Tribhuvan University, Kirtipur, Kathmandu.
Campbell, L. and Gill, G.J., (1991) *Participatory Rural Appraisal for Nepal: Concepts and Methods: a guide to the slide presentation*, HMG Ministry of Agriculture-Winrock International, Kathmandu, February.
Carruthers, I.D., (1977) 'Review of Squire and van der Tak', (paperback edition), in *Journal of Agricultural Economics*, Vol. 28, No. 1.
Carruthers, I.D. and Clayton, E.S., (1977) 'Ex post evaluation of agricultural projects – its implication for planning', *Journal of Agricultural Economics*, Vol. 28, No. 3.
Carruthers, I. and Chambers, R., (1981) 'Rapid Appraisal for Rural Development', *Agricultural Administration*, 8, 6 pp. 407–422.
Cassen, R. and Associates (1986) *Does Aid Work?*, Clarendon Press, Oxford.
Cernea, M. (ed.) (1985) *Putting People First: Sociological Variables in Rural Development*, published for the World Bank, Oxford University Press, Oxford. (Second edition, revised and expanded, 1991.)
Chabala, H.A., Kiiru, D.H., Mukuna, S.W. and Leonard, D.K., (1973) 'An Evaluation of the Programming and Implementation Management (PIM) System', Working Paper No. 89, Institute for Development Studies, University of Nairobi, March.
Chambers, R., (1969) 'Executive capacity as a scarce resource', *International Development Review*, Vol. 11, No. 2, June.
— (1974) *Managing Rural Development: Ideas and Experience from East Africa*, Scandinavian Institute of African Studies, Uppsala, reprinted 1985 by Kumarian Press, West Hartford, Connecticut.

— (1981a) 'Rural Poverty Unperceived: Problems and Remedies', *World Development*, Vol. 9, No. 1, pp. 1–9.
— (1981b) 'Introduction', in Chambers, Longhurst and Pacey *Seasonal Dimensions to Rural Poverty*, Frances Pinter, London, pp. 1–8.
— (1983) *Rural Development: Putting the Last First*, Longman, Harlow.
— (1986), 'Sustainable Livelihood Thinking: an Approach to Poverty, Environment and Development', IDS, Sussex, June.
— (1987) 'Sustainable Rural Livelihoods: A Strategy for People, Environment and Development', *Commissioned Study* **7**, Institute of Development Studies, Brighton, Sussex.
— (1988) 'Bureaucratic reversals and local diversity', *IDS Bulletin* Vol. 19, No. 4, pp. 50–56.
— (1990) *Microenvironments Unobserved*, Gatekeeper Series 22, IIED, London.
— (1992a) Rural Appraisal: Rapid, Relaxed and Participatory, *IDS Discussion Paper* No. 331, Institute of Development Studies, Brighton, Sussex, October.
— (1992b) 'The Self-Deceiving State' in Robin Murray (ed.) *New Forms of Public Administration, IDS Bulletin* Vol. 23, No. 4, pp. 31–42.
Chambers, R., Longhurst, R., Bradley, D. and Feachem, R., (1979) 'Seasonal Dimensions to Rural Poverty: Analysis and Practical Implications', *Journal of Tropical Medicine and Hygiene*, Vol. 82, No. 8, August, pp. 156–171. Also *IDS Discussion Paper* 142, Institute of Development Studies, Brighton, Sussex, February.
Chambers, R., Longhurst, R. and Pacey, A., (eds), (1981) *Seasonal Dimensions to Rural Poverty*, Frances Pinter, London.
Chambers, R. and Ghildyal, B.P., (1985) 'Agricultural Research for Resource-Poor Farmers: the farmer-first-and-last model', *Agricultural Administration*, Vol. 20, No. 1, pp. 1–30.
Chambers, R. and Jiggins, J., (1986) 'Agricultural Research for Resource-poor Farmers: a Parsimonious Paradigm', *IDS Discussion Paper* No 220, Institute of Development Studies, Brighton, Sussex.
Chambers, R. and Longhurst, R., (1986) 'Trees, Seasons and the Poor' in Longhurst (ed.) *Seasonality and Poverty*, IDS Bulletin, Vol. 17 No. 3, pp. 44–50.
Chambers, R., Pacey, A. and Thrupp, L.A., (eds), (1989) *Farmer First: farmer innovation and agricultural research*, Intermediate Technology Publications, London.
Chambers, R., Saxena, N.C. and Shah, T., (1989) *To the Hands of the Poor: Water and Trees*, Oxford and IBH, New Delhi, and Intermediate Technology Publications, London.
Cheatle, R.J. and Njoroge, J. (1991) 'Smallholder Adoption of Composting and Double Digging: an NGO approach to environmental conservation', paper for the workshop Environment and the Poor, Soil and Water Management for Sustainable Smallholder Development, The Aberdares, Arusha and Nairobi, 31 May to 12 June, 1991.
Chege, M., (1973) 'Systems Management and the Plan Implementation Process in Kenya', *Discussion Paper* No. 179, Institute for Development Studies, University of Nairobi.
Chen, M.A., (1991) *Coping with Seasonality and Drought*, Sage Publications, New Delhi, Newbury Park, London.
Chenery, H., Ahluwalia, S., Bell, C.L.G., Duloy, J.H. and Jolly, R., (1974) *Redistribution with Growth*, Oxford University Press.
Chowdhury, A.K.M. Alauddin and Chen, L.C., (1977) 'The Dynamics of Contemporary Famine', paper for the International Population Conference, Mexico, 1977, International Union for the Scientific Study of Population.

Chowdhury, A.K.M. Alauddin, Huffman, S.A. and Chen, L.C., (1981) 'Agriculture and Nutrition in Matlab Thana, Bangladesh', in Chambers, Longhurst and Pacey *Seasonal Dimensions to Rural Poverty*, Frances Pinter, London, pp. 52–61.

Cleveland, D.A. and Soleri, D., (1991) *Food from Dryland Gardens: an ecological, nutritional and social approach to small-scale household food production*, Center for People, Food and Environment, Tucson, Arizona 85701 (with support from UNICEF).

Colclough, C. and Manor, J., (eds) (1991) *States or Markets? Neo-liberalism and the Development Policy Debate*, Clarendon Press, Oxford.

Cole-King, S., (1979) 'Primary Health Care and the Role of Foreign Aid', *IDS Communication* 123, Institute of Development Studies, Brighton, Sussex.

Collins, P., (1974) 'The working of Tanzania's rural development fund: a problem in decentralization' in A.H. Rweyemamu and B.U. Mwansasu (eds), *Planning in Tanzania: Background to Decentralization*, East African Literature Bureau, Nairobi, Kampala, Dar es Salaam.

Conroy, C. and Litvinoff (eds) (1988) *The Greening of Aid: Sustainable Livelihoods in Practice*, Earthscan Publications, London.

Conway, G.R., (1985a) 'Agroecosystem Analysis', *Agricultural Administration* Vol. 20, pp. 31–55.

— (1985b) *Rapid Appraisal for Agrosystem Analysis*, Aga Khan Rural Support programme, Babar Road, Gilgit, Northern Pakistan and Centre for Environmental Technology, Imperial College of Science and Technology, London September.

— (1986) *Agroecosystem Analysis for Research and Development*, Winrock International Institute for Agricultural Development, PO Box 1172, Nana Post Office, Bangkok 10112.

— (1989) 'Diagrams for Farmers' in Chambers, Pacey and Thrupp (eds) *Farmer First*, Intermediate Technology Publications, London, pp. 77–86.

Corbett, J., (1988) 'Famine and household coping strategies', *World Development*, Vol. 16 No. 9, pp. 1099–1112.

Cornia, G.A., Jolly, R. and Stewart, F., (eds) (1987) *Adjustment with a Human Face: Volume 1 – Protecting the Vulnerable and Promoting Growth*, Clarendon Press, Oxford.

Cross, N., (1992) 'Small is Neat: the influence of niche NGOs on policy and practice', in Edwards and Hulme (eds) *Making a Difference*, Earthscan, London.

Cutting, W.A.M., (1981) 'Diarrhoeal Diseases: Rotavirus Infection in Children', in Chambers, Longhurst and Pacey *Seasonal Dimensions to Rural Poverty*, Frances Pinter, London, pp. 111–112.

Dahl, G., (1979) *Suffering Grass: Subsistence and Society of Waso Borana*, Department of Social Anthropology, University of Stockholm.

Dasgupta, B., (1975) 'A typology of Village Socio-Economic Systems from Indian Village Studies', *Economic and Political Weekly*, Vol. 10, No. 10, August, pp. 33–5.

de Waal, A.W.L., (1989) *The Famine That Kills: Darfur, Sudan, 1984–85*, Clarendon Press, Oxford.

Diab, M., (1988) 'Famines and household coping strategies in sub-Saharan Africa', final report to IDRC (IDS, Sussex, mimeo).

Dore, R., (1976) *The Diploma Disease: Education, Qualification and Development*, George Allen and Unwin, London.

Drabek, A.G., (ed) (1987) *Development Alternatives: The Challenge for NGOs, World Development Vol. 15 Supplement*, Autumn.

Drasar, B.S., Tomkins, A.M. and Feachem, R.G., (1981) 'Diarrhoeal Diseases', in Chambers, Longhurst and Pacey *Seasonal Dimensions to Rural Poverty*, Frances Pinter, London, pp. 102–111.

Dreze, J., (1990) 'Poverty in India and the IRDP Delusion', *Economic and Political Weekly* September 29 pp. A95–A104.

Dyson, T. and Crook, N., (1981) 'Causes of Seasonal Fluctuations in Vital Events', in Chambers, Longhurst and Pacey *Seasonal Dimensions to Rural Poverty*, Frances Pinter, London, pp. 135–141.

Edwards, M. and Hulme, D., (1992) 'Scaling up NGO impact on development: learning from experience', *Development in Practice*, Vol. 2, No. 2, pp. 77–91.

Edwards, M. and Hulme, D., (eds) (1992) *Making a Difference: NGOs and development in a changing world*, Earthscan, London.

Elliott, C.M., (1970) 'Effects of Human Ill-Health on Agricultural Productivity in Zambia', in A.H. Bunting, *Change in Agriculture*, Duckworth, London, pp. 647–55.

— (1980) 'Economic Aspects of Village health', *Proceedings of the Royal Society*, London, B209, pp. 71–82.

— (1982) 'The Political Economy of Sewage', *Mazingira*, Vol. 6, No. 4, pp. 44–56.

— (1987) 'Some Aspects of Relations Between the North and South in the NGO Sector', in Drabek (ed.) *Development Alternatives, World Development*, Vol. 15 Supplement, pp. 57–68.

ERCS (1988) *Rapid Rural Appraisal: a closer look at rural life in Wollo*, Ethiopian Red Cross Society, Addis Ababa and IIED, London.

Farmer, B.H., (1957) *Pioneer Peasant Colonization in Ceylon: a Study in Asian Agrarian Problems*, Oxford University Press, London.

Farrington, J., (ed.) (1988) *Experimental Agriculture*, Vol. 24, Part 3.

Farrington, J. and Martin, A., (1987) Farmer Participatory Research: a Review of Concepts and Practices, *Discussion Paper* 19, Agricultural Administration (Research and Extension) Network, Overseas Development Institute, London, June.

— (1988) Farmer participation in agricultural research: a review of concepts and practices, *Agricultural Administration Unit Occasional Paper* 9, Overseas Development Institute, London.

FAO (1986) *FAO Trade Yearbook*, FAO, Rome.

FARMIIS (1987) *Farm and Resource Management Institute Information Service Newsletter*, Farm and Resource Management Institute, Visca, Baybay, Leyte, Philippines, December.

Forsyth, R.S., (1991) 'Towards a Grounded Morality', *Changes* Vol. 9, No. 4, Morality and Method: II, pp. 264–278.

Fowler, A., (1991) 'Building partnerships between Northern and Southern development NGOs: issues for the 1990s' *Development in Practice* Vol. 1, No. 1, pp. 5–18.

Garrett, J., and Walker, S.D., (1969) *Management by Objectives in the Civil Service*, CAS Occasional Paper No. 10, HMSO, London.

Ghodake, R.D., Ryan, J.G. and Sarin, R., (1978) 'Human Labour Use in Existing and Prospective Technologies of the Semi-Arid Tropics of Peninsular India', *ICRISAT Progress Report, Economics Programme* – 1 (Village Level Studies Series 1.3), International Crops Research Institute for the Semi-Arid Tropics, Andhra Pradesh, India, December.

Gill, G.J., (1991a) *Seasonality and Agriculture in the Developing World: a problem of the poor and powerless*, Cambridge University Press, Cambridge, New York, Port Chester, Melbourne, Sydney.

— (1991b) 'But how does it compare with the Real Data?' *RRA Notes* 14 pp. 5–14 (Also *Research Report Series* Number 16, HMG Ministry of Agriculture-Winrock International, Kathmandu, January 1992).

— (1992) *Policy Analysis for Agricultural Resource Management in Nepal: a comparison of conventional and participatory approaches*, Research Support Series No. 9, HMG Ministry of Agriculture, Winrock Int., Kathmandu, July.

— (1993) *O.K., The Data's Lousy, But It's All We've Got (Being a Critique of Conventional Methods)*, Gatekeeper Series 38, IIED, London.

Gittinger, J. Price, (1982) *Economic Analysis of Agricultural Projects*, Second Edition, Economic Development Institute, World Bank, Washington DC.

Gordon, G., (1986) 'Seasonality in a Savanna District of Ghana – Perceptions of Women and Health Workers' in Longhurst (ed.) *Seasonality and Poverty*, IDS Bulletin Vol. 17, No. 3, pp. 51–57.

Government Affairs Institute (1976) *Managing Planned Agricultural Development*, (a reference book prepared for the Agency for International Development), (Agricultural Sector Implementation Programme, Washington, DC, August.

Grandstaff, S., Grandstaff, T.B., Limpinuntana, V., Simaraks, S., Smutkupt, S. and Subhadhira, S., (1990) *Report of an International Training Workshop*, held in Northeast Thailand April-May 1990, Southeast Asian Universities Agroecosystem Network, Khon Kaen University.

Gubbels, P., (1988) 'Peasant Farmer Agricultural Self-development', *Participatory Technology Development, ILEIA Newsletter* Vol. 4, No. 3, pp. 11–14.

Gueye, B., et Schoonmaker Freudenberger, K., (1990) *Introduction a la Methode Acceleree de Recherche Participative (MARP)*, Centre de Recherches pour le Developpement International, BP 2435, Dakar, Senegal, Octobre.

Guijt, I. and Pretty, J.N., (1992) *Participatory Rural Appraisal for Farmer Participatory Research in Punjab, Pakistan*, IIED, London.

GUP (1979) *'78 of GUP*, Gono Unnayan Prochesta (People's Development Efforts), Rajoir Thana, Bangladesh.

Gupta, A., (1987) 'Organising the Poor Client Responsive Research System: Can Tail Wag the Dog?', paper for the Conference on Farmers and Agricultural Research: Complementary Methods, Institute of Development Studies, Brighton, Sussex, 26–31 July.

Gupta, A.K. and IDS Workshop (1989) 'Maps Drawn by Farmers and Extensionists' in Chambers, Pacey and Thrupp (eds) *Farmer First*, Intermediate Technology Publications, London, pp. 86–92.

Gypmantasiri, Phrek *et al.*, (1980) *An Interdisciplinary Perspective of Cropping Systems in the Chiang Mai Valley: Key Questions for Research*, Faculty of Agriculture, University of Chiang Mai, Thailand.

Halstead, S.B., (1966) 'Mosquito-borne haemorrhagic fevers of South and South-East Asia', *Bulletin of the World Health Organization*, 35, pp. 3–15.

Hamnett, I., (1970) 'A Social Scientist among Technicians', *Bulletin* Vol. 3, No 1, pp. 24–9, Institute of Development Studies, Brighton, Sussex.

Harberger, A.C., (1972) *Project Evaluation: Collected Papers*, Macmillan, London.

Harrison, P., (1987) *The Greening of Africa*, Paladin Books, London.

Harvey, C., (1986) 'On the art of giving economic advice: tactics, access, damage-limitation, packaging, confessed ignorance and timing', *Public Administration and Development*, Vol. 6, pp. 445–54.

— (ed.) (1988) *Agricultural Pricing Policy in Africa: Four Country Case Studies*, Macmillan, London and Basingstoke.

Harvey, J. and Potten, D., (1987) 'Rapid Rural Appraisal of Small Irrigation Schemes in Zimbabwe', *Agricultural Administration and Extension*, 27, pp. 141–55.

Haswell, M., (1975) *The Nature of Poverty: a Case History of the First Quarter-Century after World War II*, London and Basingstoke: Macmillan.

— (1981) 'Food Consumption in Relation to Labour Output', in Chambers, Longhurst and Pacey *Seasonal Dimensions to Rural Poverty*, Frances Pinter, London, pp. 38–41.

Hedlund, H., (ed.), (1988) *Co-operatives Revisited*, Seminar Proceedings No. 21, Scandinavian Institute of African Studies, Uppsala.

Heinrich, G.M., Worman, F. and Koketso, C., (1991) 'Integrating FPR with Conventional On-Farm Research Programs: An Example from Botswana', *Journal for Farming Systems Research-Extension*, Vol. 2, No. 2, pp. 1–13.

Heyer, J., (1989) 'Landless agricultural labourers' asset strategies', *IDS Bulletin*, Vol. 20, No. 2, April.

Hirschman, A.O., (1967) *Development Projects Observed*, The Brookings Institutions, Washington, DC.

Humble, J.W., (1969) *Improving Business Results*, McGraw-Hill, New York.

Hunter, J.M., (1967) 'Seasonal Hunger in a Part of the West African Savanna: a Survey of Bodyweights in Nangodi, North East Ghana', *Transactions and Papers of the Institute of British Geographers* (Publication No. 41), pp. 167–85.

Huss-Ashmore, R. with Curry, J.J. and Hitchcock, R.K. (eds) (1988) *Coping with Seasonal Constraints*, MASCA Research Papers in Science and Archaeology, The University Museum, University of Pennsylvania, Philadelphia.

ICRISAT (1991) *Participatory Research with Women Farmers*, video, ICRISAT, Hyderabad, India.

IDRC (1980) *Nutritional Status of the Rural Population of the Sahel*, International Development Research Centre, Ottawa, Canada.

IDS (1979) 'Rural Development: Whose Knowledge Counts?', *IDS Bulletin*, Vol. 10, No. 2, Institute of Development Studies, Brighton, Sussex, January.

— (1989) 'Vulnerability: How the Poor Cope', *IDS Bulletin*, Vol. 20, No. 2, April.

Ilchman, Warren and Norman Uphoff (1971) *The Political Economy of Change*, University of California Press, Los Angeles.

ILEIA (1985–) *ILEIA Newsletter*, ILEIA, Netherlands.

ILEIA (1989) *Participatory Technology Development: A Selection of Publications*, ILEIA, Netherlands.

Irvin, G., (1976) *Modern Cost-Benefit Methods: Financial, Economic and Social Appraisal*, draft edition, The Hague: Institute of Social Studies.

Jamieson, N., (1987) 'The Paradigmatic Significance of Rapid Rural Appraisal', in *Proceedings of the 1985 International Conference on Rapid Rural Appraisal*, Khon Kaen University, Khon Kaen, Thailand, pp. 89–102.

Jayakaran, R., (1991) *Management Training Manual*, Krishi Gram Vikas Kendra, Ranchi, Bihar.

Jiggins, J., (1982) *A Report on the Regional Workshop on Seasonal Variations in the Provisioning, Nutrition and Health of Rural Families*, African Medical Research Foundation, Nairobi.

— (1986) 'Women and Seasonality: Coping with Crisis and Calamity', in Longhurst ed. *Seasonality and Poverty*, IDS Bulletin, Vol. 17, No. 3, pp. 9–18.

Jintrawet, A., Smutkupt, S., Wongsemun, C., Katawetin R. and Kerdsuk, V., (1985) *Extension activities for peanuts after rice in Ban Sum Jan, Northeast Thailand: a case study in farmer-to-farmer extension methodology*, Farming Systems Research Project, Khon Kaen University, Thailand, June.

Jodha, N.S., (1988) 'Poverty Debate in India: A Minority View', *Economic and Political Weekly*, special number, November, pp. 2421–8.

Johnson, A.W., (1972) 'Individuality and Experimentation in Traditional Agriculture', *Human Ecology*, Vol. 1, No 2, pp. 149–159.

Kajese, K., (1987) 'An Agenda of Future Tasks for International and Indigenous NGOs: Views From the South' in Drabek (ed.) *Development Alternatives*, World Development, Vol. 15, pp. 79–85.

Kenya Government (1971) *Report of the Commission of Enquiry (Public Service) Structure and Remuneration Commission) 1970–71*, (The Ndegwa Commission Report), Government Printer, Nairobi.

Khon Kaen University (1987) *Proceedings of the 1985 International Conference on Rapid Rural Appraisal*, Rural Systems Research and Farming Systems Research Projects, Khon Kaen, Thailand.

King, J.A. Jr., (1967) *Economic Development Projects and Their Appraisal: Cases and Principles from the Experience of the World Bank*, The Johns Hopkins University Press, Baltimore.

Korten, D.C., (1980) 'Community organization and rural development: a learning process approach', *Public Administration Review*, 40, pp. 480–510, Sept–Oct.

— (1984a), 'People-centred development: toward a framework', in D.C. Korten and R. Klauss (eds), *People-Centered Development*, Kumarian Press, West Hartford Connecticut, pp. 299–309.

— (1984b) 'Rural development programming: the learning process approach', in Korten and Klauss (eds) *People-Centered Development*, Kumarian Press, West Hartford, Connecticut, pp. 176–88.

— (ed.) (1987) *Community Management: Asian Experience and Perspectives*, Kumarian Press, West Hartford Connecticut.

— (1990) *Getting to the 21st Century: Voluntary Action and the Global Agenda*, Kumarian Press, West Hartford, Connecticut.

Korten, D.C. and Klauss, R., (eds) (1984) *People-Centered Development: Contributions toward theory and planning frameworks*, Kumarian Press, West Hartford, Connecticut.

Kuhn, T., (1962) *The Structure of Scientific Revolutions*, University of Chicago Press.

Kumar, S., (1991) 'Anantapur Experiment in PRA Training', *RRA Notes* 13, pp. 112–117.

Laframboise, H.L., (1971) 'Administrative Reform in the Federal Public Service: signs of a saturation psychosis', *Canadian Public Administration*, Vol. 14, No. 3, pp. 303–325.

Leakey, C., (1986) 'Biomass, Man and Seasonality in the Tropics', in Longhurst (ed.) *Seasonality and Poverty* pp. 36–43.

Lecomte, B., (1986) *Project Aid: Limitations and Alternatives*, Development Centre of the OECD, Paris.

Ledesma, A.J., (1977) 'The Sumagaysay Family: a Case Study of Landless Rural Workers', *Land Tenure Centre Newsletter*, No. 55, Land Tenure Centre, University of Wisconsin, January-March.

Lele, U., (1975) *The Design of Rural Development: Lessons from Africa*, The Johns Hopkins University Press, Baltimore and London.

Lericollais, A., (1972) 'Sob: étude géographique d'un terroir sérèr (Sénégal)', ORSTOM Atlas des Structures Agraires au sud du Sahara, No. 7, Mouton, Paris.

Leys, C., (ed.), (1969) *Politics and Change in Developing Countries: Studies in theory and practice of development*, Cambridge University Press.

Lightfoot, C., de Guia Jr., O. and Ocado, F., (1988) 'A Participatory Method for Systems-Problem Research: Rehabilitating Marginal Uplands in the Philippines', *Experimental Agriculture*, 24, Part 3, pp. 301–309.

Lightfoot, C., de Guia Jr., O., Aliman, A. and Ocado, F., (1989) 'Systems diagrams to help farmers decide in on-farm research' in Chambers, Pacey and Thrupp (eds) *Farmer First*, Intermediate Technology Publications, London, pp. 93–105.

Lightfoot, C., Axinn, N., John, K.C., Chambers, R., Singh, R.K., Garrity, D., Singh, V.P., Mishra, P. and Salman, A. (1991) *Training Resource Book for Participatory Experimental Design*, NDUAT, Faizabad, India, ICLARM, Philippines and IRRI, Philippines.

Lightfoot, C., Noble, R. and Morales, R., (1991) *Training Resource Book on a Participatory Method for Modelling Bioresource Flows*, ICLARM, Philippines.

Lightfoot, C., Feldman, S. and Zainul Abedin, M., (1991) *Households, Agro-ecosystems and Rural Resources Management: A guidebook for broadening the concepts of gender and farming systems*, Bangladesh Agricultural Research Institute, Bangladesh and ICLARM, Philippines.

Lipton, M., (1977) *Why Poor People Stay Poor: A Study of Urban Bias in World Development*, Temple Smith, London.
— (1986) 'Seasonality and Ultrapoverty', in Longhurst (ed.) *Seasonality and Poverty*, IDS Bulletin, Vol. 17, pp. 4–8.
Little, I.M.D. and Mirrlees, J.A., (1974) *Project Appraisal and Planning for Developing Countries*, Heinemann Education Books, London.
Longhurst, R., (1979) 'Malnutrition and the community – the social origins of deprivation', *Proceedings of the Nutrition Society*, 38, pp. 11–16.
Longhurst, R., (1986) 'Household Food Strategies in Response to Seasonality and Famine', in Longhurst (ed.) *Seasonality and Poverty*, IDS Bulletin, Vol. 17, pp. 27–35.
Longhurst, R., (ed.) (1986) *Seasonality and Poverty, IDS Bulletin*, Vol. 17, No. 3 July.
Longhurst, R. and Payne, P., (1979) 'Seasonal Aspects of Nutrition: Review of Evidence and Policy Implications' *Discussion Paper* 145, Institute of Development Studies, Brighton, Sussex, September.
Lovelace, G., Subhadira, S. and Simaraks, S., (eds), (1988) *Rapid Rural Appraisal in Northeast Thailand: Case Studies*, KKU-Ford Rural Systems Research Project, Khon Kaen University, Khon Kaen, Thailand.
McCracken, J.A., (1988) *Participatory Rapid Rural Appraisal in Gujarat: a trial model for the Aga Khan Rural Support Programme (India)*, International Institute for Environment and Development, London, November.
McCracken, J.A., Pretty, J.N. and Conway, G.R., (1988) *An Introduction to Rapid Rural Appraisal for Agricultural Development*, International Institute for Environment and Development, London.
McGregor, I.A., (1976) 'Health and Communicable Disease in a Rural African Environment', *Oikos*, 27, pp. 180–92.
McGregor, I.A., Billewicz, W.Z. and Thomson, A.M., (1961) 'Growth and Mortality in Children in an African Village', *British Medical Journal*, pp. 661–6.
McKean, R.N., (1965) *Efficiency in Government Through Systems Analysis*, John Wiley and Sons, New York.
Mascarenhas, J., (1992) 'Participatory rural appraisal and participatory learning methods: recent experiences from MYRADA and South India' *Forests, Trees and People Newsletter* No. 15/16 February, pp. 10–17.
Mascarenhas, J. and Kumar, P., (1991) 'Participatory Mapping and Modelling: User's Notes' *RRA Notes* 12, pp. 9–20.
Mascarenhas, J. *et al.*, (1991) *Participatory Rural Appraisal: Proceedings of the February 1991 Bangalore PRA Trainers Workshop, RRA Notes* Number 13, IIED and MYRADA, Bangalore, August.
Mata, L.J., (1978) *The Children of Santa Maria Cauque: a Prospective Field Study of Health and Growth*, MIT Press, Cambridge, Massachusetts.
Matlon, P., Cantrell, R., King, D. and Benoit-Cattin, M. (eds) (1984), *Coming Full Circle: Farmers' Participation in the Development of Technology*, International Development Research Centre, Ottawa.
Maurya, D.M., Bottrall, A. and Farrington, J., (1988) 'Improved Livelihoods, Genetic Diversity and Farmer Participation: a strategy for rice breeding in rainfed areas of India', *Experimental Agriculture*, 24, Part 3, pp. 311–320.
Meals for Millions (1988) *Rapid Rural Appraisal for Project Analysis Planning*, Meals for Millions, Kenya.
Mellors, D.R., (1987) 'Integrated Rural Development Programme – Serenje, Mpika, Chinsali – Zambia', paper for the IIED Conference on Sustainable Development, London, 28–30 April.
Molander, C.F., (1972) 'Management by Objectives in Perspective', *Journal of Management Studies*, Vol. 9, No. 1, February, pp. 74–81.

Mollison, B., (1990) *Permaculture: A Designer's Manual*, The Deccan Development Society and Permaculture – India, Meera Apartments, Bashirbagh, Hyderabad, India, October.

Moore, M., (1991) 'Rent-seeking and Market Surrogates: the case of irrigation policy', in Colclough and Manor (eds) *States or Markets?*, Clarendon Press, Oxford, pp. 279–305.

Moris, J.R., (1970) 'Multi-Subject Farm Surveys Reconsidered: Some Methodological Issues', paper for the East African Agricultural Economics Society Conference, Dar es Salaam, 31 March to 4 April 1970.

— (1987) 'Irrigation as a Privileged Solution in African Development', *Development Policy Review*, 5, pp. 99–123.

— (1988) 'OXFAM's Kenya restocking projects', *ODI Pastoral Development Network Paper* 26c, September.

Mukherjee, N., (1992) 'Villagers' Perceptions of Rural Poverty Through the Mapping Methods of PRA', *RRA Notes* 15, pp. 21–26.

Muller, R., (1981) 'Guinea Worm Infection', in Chambers, Longhurst and Pacey *Seasonal Dimensions to Rural Poverty*, Frances Pinter, London, pp. 125–127.

NES *et al.* (n.d.), *Participatory Rural Appraisal Handbook*, National Environment Secretariat, Government of Kenya; Clark University; Egerton University; and the Center for International Development and Environment of the World Resources Institute.

Nettl, J.P., (1969) 'Strategies in the study of political development', in Colin Leys (ed.), *Politics and Change in Developing Countries*, Cambridge University Press, pp. 13–34.

Nield, T., (1986) 'Peeling off the labels', *New Scientist*, 2 January, p. 47.

Norman, D., Baker, D., Heinrich, G. and Worman, F., (1988) 'Technology Development and Farmer Groups: Experience from Botswana', *Experimental Agriculture*, 24, part 3, pp. 321–31.

ODA (1972) *A guide to Project Appraisal in Developing Countries* (Overseas Development Administration), HMSO, London.

ODI (1991) *Environmental Change and Dryland Management in Machakos District, Kenya, 1930–1990, ODI Working Papers* Numbers 53 – 63 continuing.

OECD (1973) *Methods of Project Appraisal in Developing Countries*, OECD, Paris.

OXFAM (1976) *Field Directors' Handbook*, OXFAM, Oxford.

PAG of the UN (1977) *Women in Food Production, Food Handling and Nutrition with Special Emphasis on Africa*, final report, Protein-Calorie Advisory Group (PAG) of the United Nations System, United Nations, New York.

Palmer, I., (1981) 'Seasonal Dimensions of Womens' Roles', in Chambers, Longhurst and Pacey *Seasonal Dimensions to Rural Poverty*, Frances Pinter, London, pp. 195–201.

Parkin, D.J., (1972) *Palms, Wine and Witnesses: Public Spirit and Private Gain in an African Farming Community*, Intertext Books, London.

Pearse, A., (1977) 'Technology and peasant production: reflections on a global study', *Development and Change*, July.

Peters, T., (1987) *Thriving on Chaos: handbook for a management revolution*, Pan Books in association with Macmillan, London.

Peters, T.J. and Waterman, R.H., (1982) *In Search of Excellence: Lessons from America's Best-Run Companies*, Harper and Row, New York.

PID and NES (1989) *An Introduction to Participatory Rural Appraisal for Rural Resources Management*, Program for International Development, Clark University, Worcester, Mass and National Environment Secretariat, Ministry of Environment and Natural Resources, Nairobi, November.

Porter, D., Allen, B. and Thompson, G., (1991) *Development in Practice: paved with good intentions*, Routledge, London and New York.

134

Porter, M.J., (1981) 'Infectious Skin Diseases', in Chambers, Longhurst and Pacey *Seasonal Dimensions to Rural Poverty*, Frances Pinter, London, pp. 114–116.

Pottier, J., (1991) 'Representation and Accountability: Understanding social change through rapid appraisal with reference to Northern Zambia', typescript, Department of Social Anthropology, SOAS, University of London, April.

Pratt, B. and Boyden, J., (eds), (1985) *The Field Directors' Handbook: and OXFAM manual for development workers*, OXFAM, Oxford.

Prescott, N.M., (1979) 'The Economics of Malaria, Filariasis and Trypanosomiasis', typescript, Magdalen College, Oxford, February.

Pretty, J.N., (1990) *Rapid Catchment Analysis for Extension Agents: notes on the 1990 Kericho training workshop for the Ministry of Agriculture, Kenya*, IIED, November.

Quiros, C.A., Gracia, T. and Ashby, J.A., (1991) *Farmer Evaluations of Technology: Methodology for Open-ended Evaluation*, CIAT, July.

Rahmato, D., (1987) 'Peasant survival strategies', in Angela Penrose (ed.) *Beyond the Famine: an examination of the issues behind famine in Ethiopia*, International Institute for Relief and Development, Food for the Hungry International, Geneva, pp. 1–26.

Reddin, W.J., (1971) *Effective MBO*, Management Publications Limited, London.

Reij, C., Cullis, A. and Aklilu, Y., (1987) 'Soil and Water Conservation in sub-Saharan Africa: the Need for a Bottom-up Approach', paper for the OXFAM Arid Lands Management Workshop, Cotonou, 23–27 March.

Reijntjes, C., Haverkort, B. and Waters-Bayer, A., (1992) *Farming for the Future: an introduction to low-external-input and sustainable agriculture*, Macmillan, London and Basingstoke and ILEIA, Netherlands.

Repetto, R., (1986) *Skimming the Water: Rent-seeking and the Performance of Public Irrigation Systems*, Research Report 4, World Resources Institute, Washington DC.

Republic of Botswana (1976) *Planning Officers' Manual* (Ministry of Finance and Development Planning, printed by the Government Printer, Gaborone, August).

Repulda, R., Quero Jr, F.V., Ayaso III, R.B., de Guia Jr., O. and Lightfoot, C., (1987) 'Doing Research with Resource Poor Farmers: FSDP-EV Perspectives and Programs', paper for the Conference on Farmers and Agricultural Research: Complementary Methods, 26–31 July, Institute of Development Studies, Brighton, Sussex, July.

Rhoades, R.E., (1984a) 'Tecnicista versus campesinista: praxis and theory of farmer involvement in agricultural research', in Matlon *et al.* (eds). *Coming Full Circle: Farmers' Participation in the Development of Technology*, International Development Research Centre, Ottawa pp. 139–150.

— (1984b), *Breaking New Ground: Agricultural Anthropology*, International Potato Center, Lima.

— (1987) 'Farmers and experimentation', *Discussion Paper* No 21, Agricultural Administration (Research and Extension) Network, Overseas Development Institute, London, December.

— (1989) 'The Role of Farmers in the Creation of Agricultural Technology', in Chambers, Pacey and Thrupp (eds) *Farmer First*, Intermediate Technology Publications, London, pp. 3–9.

Rhoades, R.E. and Booth, R.H., (1982) 'Farmer-Back-to-Farmer: a Model for Generating Acceptable Agricultural Technology', *Agricultural Administration*, Vol. 11, pp. 127–137.

Rhoades, R.E., Sandoval, V.N. and Bagalanon, C.P., (1990) *Asian Training of Trainers on Farm Household Diagnostic Skills*, November 11–18, 1990 International Potato Center User's Perspective with Agricultural Research and

135

Development (UPWARD) and Institute of Forest Conservation, University of the Philippines at Los Banos.

Richards, P., (1985) *Indigenous Agricultural Revolution: Ecology and Food Production in West Africa*, Hutchinson, London.

Robertson, J., (1983), *The Sane Alternative: a Choice of Futures*, James Robertson, The Old Bakehouse, Cholsey, nr. Wallingford, Oxford.

— (1985), *Future Work: Jobs, self-employment and leisure after the industrial age*, Gower/Maurice Temple Smith, Aldershot.

Roe, E. and Fortmann, L. (1982) *Season and Strategy: the Changing Organization of the Rural Water Sector in Botswana*, Special Series on Resource Management No 1, Rural Development Committee, Center for International Studies, Cornell University, Ithaca, NY.

Rondinelli, D.A., (1976a) 'International requirements for project preparation: aids or obstacles to development planning', *Journal of the American Institute of Planners*, Vol. 42, No. 3, July. (Version cited here is a pre-publication mimeography, not dated.)

— (1976b) 'International assistance policy and development project administration: the impact of imperious rationality', *International Organization*, Vol. 30, No. 4, Autumn.

— (1983) *Development Projects as Policy Experiments: An Adaptive Approach to Development Administration*, London and New York: Methuen.

Rowland, M.G.M. *et al.*, (1981) 'Seasonality and the Growth of Infants in a Gambian Village', in Chambers, Longhurst and Pacey *Seasonal Dimensions to Rural Poverty*, Frances Pinter, London, pp. 164–175.

RRA Notes, (1988–) Numbers 1–16 continuing, International Institute for Environment and Development, 3 Endsleigh Street, London WC1H ODD, 1988– especially Number 13 (see Mascarenhas *et al.* 1991).

Sahn, D.E. (ed.), (1989) *Seasonal Variability in Third World Agriculture: the Consequences for Food Security*, Johns Hopkins Press, Baltimore.

Schaffer, B.B., (1969) 'The Deadlock in Development Administration', in Leys ed. *Politics and Change in Developing Countries*, Cambridge University Press.

Scheuermeier, U., (1988) *Approach Development: a contribution to participatory development of techniques based on a practical experience in Tinau Watershed Project, Nepal*, LBL, Landwirtschaftliche Beratungszentrale, CH–8315 Lindau, Switzerland.

Schumacher, E.F., (1973) *Small is Beautiful: a study of economics as if people mattered*, Blond and Briggs, London.

Schofield, S., (1974) 'Seasonal Factors Affecting Nutrition in Different Age Groups and especially Pre-school Children', *Journal of Development Studies*, Vol. 11, No. 1, October.

— (1979) *Development and the Problems of Village Nutrition*, Croom Helm, London.

Scoones, I. and Thompson, J., (1992) 'Rural People's Knowledge, Agricultural Research and Extension Practice: Towards a theoretical framework', Beyond Farmer First Overview, Paper No. 1, IIED/IDS Conference, Beyond Farmer First, 27–29 October, IIED, March.

Scott, M.F.G., MacArthur, J.D., and Newbery, D.M.G., (1976) *Project Appraisal in Practice: The Little-Mirrlees Method Applied in Kenya*, Heinemann Educational Books, London.

Seers, D. and Joy, L., (eds), (1971) *Development in a Divided World*, Penguin.

Self, P., (1975) *Econocrats and the Policy Process: The Politics and Philosophy of Cost-Benefit Analysis*, London: Macmillan.

Shah, A.C., (1991) 'Shoulder Tapping: a technique of training in participatory rural appraisal' *Forests, Trees and People Newsletter*, No 14, pp. 14–15.

136

Shah, P., Bharadwaj, G. and Ambastha, R., (1991) 'Farmers as Analysts and Facilitators in Participatory Rural Appraisal and Planning', *RRA Notes* 13, pp. 84–94.

Sheldrake, R., (1985) *A New Science of Life: The Hypothesis of Formative Causation*, (Second edition) Anthony Blond, London.

Simmons, E.B., (1981) 'A Case Study in Food Production, Sale and Distribution', in Chambers, Longhurst and Pacey *Seasonal Dimensions to Rural Poverty*, Frances Pinter, London, pp. 73–80.

Singer, H., (1950), 'Distribution of Gains between Investing and Borrowing Countries', *American Economic Review, Papers and Proceedings*, Vol. 40, (May) 1950, pp. 473–85.

Squire, L. and van der Tak, H.G., (1975) *Economic Analysis of Projects*, The Johns Hopkins University Press, Baltimore and London.

Ssennyonga, J.W., (1976) 'The Cultural Dimensions of Demographic Trends', *Populi*, Vol. 3, No. 2, pp. 2–11.

Streeten, P., (1983) 'Development Dichotomies', *World Development*, Vol. 11, No. 10, October, pp. 875–89.

Sumberg, J. and Okali, C. (1988) 'Farmers, On-farm Research and the Development of new Technology', *Experimental Agriculture* 24, Part 3, pp. 333–342.

Swift, J., (1981) 'Labour and Subsistence in a Pastoral Economy', in Chambers, Longhurst and Pacey *Seasonal Dimensions to Rural Poverty*, Frances Pinter, London, pp. 80–87.

Theis, J. and McGrady, H., (1991) *Participatory Rapid Appraisal for Community Development: a training manual based on experiences in the Middle East and North Africa*, IIED and Save the Children Federation.

Thomson, A.M., (1988) 'Zimbabwe', in Harvey (ed.) *Agricultural Pricing Policy in Africa*, Macmillan, London and Basingstoke, pp. 186–219.

Tomkins, A., (1981) 'Seasonal Health Problems in the Zaria Region', in Chambers, Longhurst and Pacey *Seasonal Dimensions to Rural Poverty*, Frances Pinter, London, pp. 177–182.

Toulmin, C., (1986) 'Access to Food, Dry Season Strategies and Household Size amongst the Bambara of Central Mali' in Longhurst (ed.) *Seasonality and Poverty*, IDS Bulletin, Vol. 17, pp. 58–66.

Tung, L. and Balina, F.T., (1988) *Proceedings: Philippines Upland Research and Extension Training Workshop*, June 19–24, 1988, ATI, NTC-Visayas, Visca, Baybay, Leyte, Philippines, June.

Uphoff, N., (1985) 'Fitting Projects to People', in M. Cernea (ed.), *Putting People First*, Oxford University Press, New York, pp. 359–95.

— (1988) 'Paraprojects as New Modes of International Assistance for Self-sustainable Development in the 1990s'. Supplementary paper for the Colloquium on The Changing Nature of Poverty in the 1990s: a policy perspective, Michigan State University, March 1988, revised 10 May.

Valmayor, R.V. and Mamon, C.R., (1987) 'Research Information Systems for Agriculture and Natural Resources in the Philippines', in ISNAR *International Workshop on Agriculture Research Management*, The Hague, Netherlands.

van Steijn, T., (1991) 'Rapid Rural Appraisal in the Philippines: report of a study on the application of RRA by Philippines NGOs, GOs and University Institutes', draft version for comment, Council for People's Development, Quezon City, Metro Manila, Philippines.

Walker, T.S. and Ryan, J.G., (1990) *Village and Household Economies in India's Semi-arid Tropics*, Johns Hopkins Press, Baltimore and London.

Walsh, J.A. and Warren, K.S., (1979) 'Selective Primary Health Care: An Interim Strategy for Disease Control in Developing Countries', The Rockefeller Foundation, New York.

Walsh, R.P.D., (1981) 'The Nature of Climatic Seasonality', in Chambers, Longhurst and Pacey *Seasonal Dimensions to Rural Poverty* pp. 11–21.

Warrell, D.A. and Arnett, C. (1978) 'The importance of Bites by the Saw-Scaled or Carpet Viper *(Echis carinatus)*: Epidemiological Studies in Nigeria and a Review of the World Literature', *Acta Tropica*, Vol 33, No. 4.

Watts, M., (1981) 'The Sociology of Seasonal Food Shortage in Hausaland', in Chambers, Longhurst and Pacey *Seasonal Dimensions to Rural Poverty*, Frances Pinter, London, pp. 201–206.

White, C., (1986) 'Food Shortages and Seasonality in WoDaaBe Communities in Niger', in Longhurst (ed.) *Seasonality and Poverty*, IDS Bulletin, Vol. 17, pp. 19–26.

Whitehead, R.G. *et al.*, (1978) 'Factors Influencing Lactation Performance in Rural Gambian Mothers', *The Lancet*, 22 July, 178–81.

Whyte, M.A., (1987) 'Crisis and recentralization: 'indigenous development' in Eastern Uganda', *Working Paper 1987/1*, Center for African Studies, University of Copenhagen.

Wolf, E.C., (1986) *Beyond the Green Revolution: New Approaches for Third World Agriculture, Worldwatch Paper* 73, Worldwatch Institute, Washington DC.

World Bank (1975) *Health Sector Policy Paper*, World Bank, Washington DC.

— (1981) *Accelerated Development in Sub-Saharan Africa: an agenda for action* (The Berg Report), World Bank, Washington DC.

— (1988) *Rural Development: World Bank experience, 1965–86*, World Bank, Washington DC.

Index

abstract thought 16
Accelerated Development in Sub-Saharan Africa (Berg Report) 109, 110
access biases 51–2
ActionAid 101
Activists for Social Alternatives 101
ACTS (African Centre for Technology Studies) 95
additionality 89, 90–7
administrative capacity 17–18, 33–5
Afghanistan 113
Aga Khan Rural Support Programme (India) 97, 98
agriculture 60–75
agroecosystem analysis 59, 97
agroforestry 7, 65
Agroforestry Systems 7
AIDS 61
analysis, farmers' 69
Angola 113
appraisal procedures 27, 32
assets, selling of 48, 49, 118–9
assimilation 6

balance sheets 93–94
Bangladesh 42, 43, 49, 53, 54, 56, 60, 95, 123–4
Belcher 45, 52
Belshaw, Deryke 24
Bentley, Jeffrey 73
Berg Report 109, 110
biases 8, 9, 51–3, 77, 78, 80
big projects 28, 30–1, 78, 82–3, 87, 115–6
block grant system 36
blueprint approach 12, 84, 93–4
Botswana 33, 58, 68, 71, 108
BRAC 95
Bunch, Roland 68, 72, 96
Bunting, Hugh 45
Bura Irrigation Project, Kenya 80
Burkina Faso 58, 79, 84, 111
Burma 60
Burns and Stalker 12
Burundi 113
Butterfield, Herbert 14

Carruthers, Ian 34, 37

CDR (complex, diverse and risk-prone) agriculture 60–75, 121
Centre for Science and Environment (New Delhi) 95
Chad 113
change, rates of 11
changing rules 120
checklists 37
children 42–4, 56
China 60, 114
choices 71, 72, 73, 120–1
cholera 48
Chowdhury 56
Clark University 97
Clayton, Eric 34
clusters of procedures 16–17, 25
collective agriculture 114–5
Colombia 68, 72, 107
communication 105–6, 120
Companiganj 43
comparative competence 89, 93–4, 97, 99, 103–4
complex, diverse and risk-prone (CDR) agriculture 60–75, 120–1
complexity 11, 19–20, 32–3, 63, 65, 74, 120–1
conservatism 4–5
consultants 24, 30, 82, 83
controls affecting the poor 116–18
Coping with Seasonality and Drought (Chen) 58
core-periphery view 4, 5, 7, 8, 77, 110–2
Cornell University 11, 86
corruption 82, 104, 111–2, 113–4
cost-benefit analysis (CBA) 4, 5, 7, 27, 30–2, 33, 34, 37–8, 80–1, 122
costs of sickness 41, 45–50
counterfactual 34, 92–3
credit 28, 34, 58, 86–7, 96, 108, 117
crops 19, 65, 71, 72, 74

'daylighting' 111
decentralization 11, 12, 35–6, 57, 73, 83–4, 120–1
decision matrices 37
delays 33, 86
dengue fever 42
Design of Rural Development: Lessons from Africa (Lele) 30

139

142